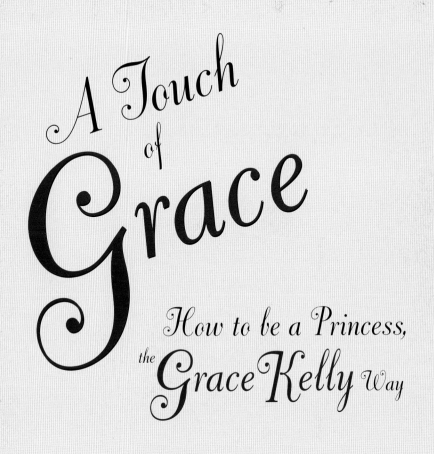

A Touch of Grace

Grace

How to be a Princess, the Grace Kelly Way

Cindy De La Hoz

RUNNING PRESS
PHILADELPHIA · LONDON

To Manny, Jess, and Michael

Printed in China

This book may not be reproduced in whole or in part, in any form or by any means, electronic or mechanical, including photocopying, recording, or by any information storage and retrieval system now known or hereafter invented, without written permission from the publisher.

9 8 7 6 5 4 3 2 1
Digit on the right indicates the number of this printing

Library of Congress Control Number: 2009905541

ISBN 978-0-7624-3804-4

Designed by Corinda Cook
Edited by Jennifer Kasius
Typography: Caslon, Dorchester Script, and Trade Gothic

Running Press Book Publishers
2300 Chestnut Street
Philadelphia, PA 19103-4371

Visit us on the web!
www.runningpress.com

Contents

Princess of Grace

Portrait of a lady, 1954.

At a cursory glance, Grace Kelly's life seemed to be a child's favorite fairytale come true. Snapshot: well-brought-up girl surrounded by beautiful family. Snapshot: movie queen accepting her Academy Award. Snapshot: breathtaking bride marrying a real-life Prince Charming. In many ways, this average-girl-turned-star-turned-princess-turned-legend brought to life our most cherished fantasies. The fact that she was as human as the rest of us, complete with flaws, makes her story all the more compelling and begs the question: How can we all attain a touch of Grace?

Crown or no crown, Grace Kelly was America's princess. Born in Philadelphia to local legend John Kelly and his attractive and educated wife, Margaret, Grace was raised to make a mark in the world in her own right. Inherent ambition led her to the top of the New York modeling world and then to top honors as an actress in Hollywood. This sense of excellence

Classic Grace with a wide-eyed gaze.

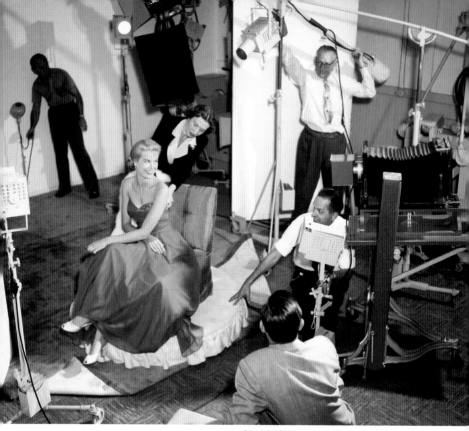

A look behind the scenes of a fashion photo session.

extended to her remarkable physical appearance, which reflected the inner beauty of a woman who touched the lives of many and who helped the principality of Monaco and its people regain their standing in the world at large.

While all eyes were on her, Grace had a way of projecting an unstudied sort of beauty, sophisticated style, and infinite poise in spite of her many private challenges. This calm under pressure had its roots in her upbringing and

JOURS DE FRANCE

GRACE DE MONACO

DIX ANS DE BONHEUR

On her tenth anniversary as Princess of Monaco.

natural gifts as an actress. Grace's cool façade became her trademark in her films as well as in her private life, as far as the public could tell. Whether she was feeling frightened, lonely, anxious, or excited, she exemplified her official title as Princess of Monaco, and the world felt she was indeed her most serene of highnesses. Those close to Grace, of course, knew the person behind the image. She was by no means a saint and never claimed to be, but she was a good person at heart.

Grace was from a prominent family that worked hard for every penny they had, and she labored to achieve her goals. Though she suffered her share of hardships, her life was indeed charmed in many ways. Grace repaid her blessings and gave back to the world, through her tireless charitable work, a small treasury of films that continues to entertain and inspire audiences, and the creation of an exemplary picture of America to the international community from her position as Princess of Monaco. Ultimately, Grace earned a rare position that she maintains today—simply that of a good role model.

This book combines biographical commentary, anecdotes, Grace Kelly's own words, and the voices of those who knew her best to highlight lessons to learn from a life well lived. She was a child of privilege in Philadelphia, an ambitious actress, model, Hollywood star, princess, wife, mother, and finally international icon of style, beauty, and dignity. The hope is that these lessons will inspire readers to feel like an everyday princess, the Grace Kelly way.

Grace's profile was beyond compare.

CHAPTER ONE

Family Matters:

Lessons from Childhood

"A nice girl from a nice family . . ."

Growing up around successful people can influence greatness. John B. Kelly was a formidable figure in Philadelphia in the early twentieth century. "Jack" was the youngest of ten children born to Irish immigrants. He started as a bricklayer, then after army service in World War I, a loan from one of his elder brothers financed the startup of his own company. Turning Kelly for Brickwork into the largest brick firm on the east coast was not Jack's greatest claim to fame, however. Training relentlessly on the Schuylkill River, he was a rowing champion who won three Olympic gold medals, two in 1920 and one in 1924. Feted as a hero in Philadelphia,

Eight-year-old Grace greets her father, John B. Kelly. She had an eye for the camera already.

Father and daughter Grace ham it up for the cameras.

he ran for mayor on the Democratic ticket in 1935. He didn't win, but his prominence in the city was not dimmed.

The exceptionalism of the Kellys was by no means limited to Jack. Grace's three uncles on her paternal side were Patrick Henry Kelly, known for building some of the most recognizable structures of Philadelphia; Walter Kelly, whose performances as the "Virginia Judge" made him a star on the vaudeville circuit; and George Kelly, the Pulitzer Prize-winning playwright of *Craig's Wife* and *The Torchbearers*.

The Kelly family vacationing in Ocean City, New Jersey. Clockwise are Grace, Margaret, John Jr., Peggy, Jack

Lizanne and Grace with their father at their summer home in Ocean City, New Jersey.

Be your own person:

Grace could easily have used her family connections to get ahead in her career, particularly at the time she was pounding the pavement of New York looking for stage work. She said, "I knew if I started trading on the reputation of my uncles to get jobs, it was a sure way to win enemies and lose out in the theater."

Being one of the "Kellys of Philadelphia" gave Grace a measure of prominence, and she had her pictures in the papers long before achieving anything in her own right. She didn't have to make any effort to attain the "famous for being famous" status of today's "celebutantes" and reality TV stars. Grace worked at being the kind of person worthy of distinction because of her achievements. To her, what you accomplish in life was far more important than who you are.

> "Never be the one who takes and gives nothing in return. Everything must be earned, through work, persistence, and sincerity."
>
> —Jack Kelly motto

Don't let them underestimate you:

Grace surprised her parents, particularly Jack, by blossoming into a world-class beauty and international icon. Aggressive and competitive, Jack often did not see eye to eye with the most sensitive of his four children, the one considered the runt of the litter, who was not athletic and perpetually had the sniffles. As she grew older and found her niche in the world, the emotional rift between them only grew. He did not approve of her chosen professional path and hoped that her dream would dissipate. Fully aware of this, Grace strived to be the best in her profession. When she reached the peak of her career, winning an Oscar for *The Country Girl*, his reaction reported by the media seemed a mix of wonder, bewilderment, and just a hint of pride.

"I hoped Grace would win. I thought her performance in *Country Girl* merited some kind of reward. But I thought Judy [Garland] might get it because of her comeback. We think Grace was very lucky, but we are sorry that both she and Judy couldn't have won."

—Jack Kelly

Grace accepts an award for her work in films from the Junior Chamber of Commerce of Philadelphia, June 1955.

Never stop trying:

Grace was ever Jack's adoring daughter and she sought to have a good relationship with him. In the late 1950s, the years prior to Jack's death from cancer in 1960 and Grace's first years as Princess of Monaco, friends say he finally began to understand his daughter better. He saw her impact on the world and respected her for the woman, wife, and mother that she had become.

Cary Grant (right) and the Kelly girls. Grace's sisters enjoy the premiere of *To Catch a Thief*, held in Philadelphia in 1955.

$\mathcal{L}$earn to forgive:

Margaret Kelly was quite an accomplished and educated woman for her time. She studied physical education at Temple University and went on to teach at the University of Pennsylvania. Grace's brother called her their "Prussian General Mother." Margaret was reared in a stiff German household and brought her children up the same way; the ability to keep emotions in check, self-discipline, and modesty remained with Grace all her life.

Grace's relationship with her mother was generally good, though it was tested quite dramatically and unexpectedly in 1956. Shortly after her daughter became engaged to Prince Rainier, Margaret gave a detailed memoir of Grace's life and loves to the Philadelphia *Bulletin*, presumably "to set the record straight," but the articles only rehashed and brought on increased speculation about her daughter's past amours. Margaret didn't think she had done wrong, and Grace couldn't stay mad at her. She moved on and forgave her mother.

"Of the four children, she's the last one I'd expect to support me in my old age."

—Jack Kelly

A portrait of Margaret Kelly with her children, John Jr., Peggy, Lizanne, and Grace.

"From the time she was a little girl—and she was a darling, so lovely I used to wish she might never grow up—there was always something a bit different, a bit withdrawn, about her. Whereas the other children—Peggy, John Jr., and Lizanne— were the extroverts, Grace was shy and retiring."

—Margaret Kelly

Margaret Kelly
with her girls—
Lizanne, age four;
Grace, eight; and
Peggy, twelve.

Grace and
Margaret Kelly in
New York, 1956.

John Jr., Grace, and Peggy, before the arrival of youngest sister Lizanne.

Holding her baby sister, Lizanne.

"She was a shy child, but there was a kind of inner tranquility and quiet resourcefulness. She never minded being in bed and would sit there with her dolls for hours on end making up little plays. Grace would change her voice for each doll, giving it a different character."

—Margaret Kelly

Accept that family is hard to please:

The Kellys could be a difficult crowd when it came to accepting newcomers. They influenced all breakups with Grace's serious boyfriends in the years before she met Prince Rainier. At the time of her daughter's engagement, Margaret Kelly said, ". . . the very last thing in my mind was the possibility of Grace ever becoming a real-life, honest-to-goodness princess." But in hindsight it would seem the Kellys would have accepted nothing less than a prince—provided he was Catholic, which indeed Rainier was.

Have faith:

The Catholic faith, nurtured in Grace from childhood, was always important to her. To ensure that she and her future husband would have common values and raise their children in the faith, it was important to Grace and essential to her family that the man she marry be a Catholic. The parish priest of St. Bridget's in Philadelphia during Grace's childhood, Father John Carlin, remained close with Grace and the Kelly family. He was on hand at her wedding in Monaco to bestow his blessing upon the newlyweds.

In most respects Grace followed the traditions of the Church, but she had her own opinion on one very important issue that remains controversial: "I'd be in favor of priests being able to marry, at least once, because I think the vocation would attract more and better men. A priest and his wife, working together, could accomplish so much."

For Grace, the Catholic faith was a mainstay in life and played a role in helping her through hardships, but she would say it need not be the same for everyone. Faith in friends and family through the difficult times functions very well indeed, regardless of creed.

Be a supportive sibling:

Jack and Margaret's first child, Peggy, was born in 1925, John Jr. came in 1927, followed by Grace on November 12, 1929, and Lizanne in 1933. All but Grace were as outgoing and robust as their father. John Jr., called "Kell," accepted the challenge of maintaining the high standards set for him by his father's accomplished generation. Grace said "The talk [at the dinner table] was mostly about rowing." Like his father, Kell became an Olympic gold-medal winner, but he was also victorious where his father had not been, becoming champion at the Diamond Sculls in Henley, England. Jack Sr.'s application to the world's leading sculling event had been rejected without explanation. Jack always

Thirteen-year-old Grace congratulates John Jr. upon becoming the national singles sculls champion, 1944.

felt it was a personal snub in the days when a man who worked with his hands, however successful, was no gentleman and not worthy of a place in the Henley Royal Regatta. Successful though he was, having his father's ambitions projected onto Kell was not easy. Grace felt for her brother and did her best to be supportive, standing by him at difficult times, including through troubled relationships and divorce from his first wife. Grace and Kell were close throughout her life.

Wishing Kell best wishes as he leaves for the Olympics in 1948.

Grace and sister Lizanne on their return from England, where brother John Jr. had just won the Diamond Sculls

Grace and Lizanne Kelly at home in Philadelphia. Grace was in town to attend her younger sister's wedding in 1955.

Have a creative outlet:

Grace was an introverted child. Unable to express herself as loudly as her more gregarious siblings, she took to writing poetry. An example of the young Grace's prose:

Little flower, you're a lucky one,
You soak in all the lovely sun.
You stand and watch it all go by
And never once do bat an eye,
While others have to fight and strain
against the world and its every pain
> *of living.*
But you must too have wars to fight—
the cold bleak darkness of every night,
of a bigger vine which seeks to grow,
and is able to stand the rain and snow,
and yet you never let it show
> *on your pretty face.*

Grace's love for the camera extended to taking pictures as well. Here she snaps a few prior to her sister Lizanne's wedding, 1955.

Come out of your shell:

Grace's timid self as a child gave way to a proper but mischievous teenager by the time she reached Stevens high school. She was the darling of the boys at Penn Charter, the prestigious prep school where her brother was enrolled, and her first love was one of his classmates, Harper Davis. Her blossoming beauty and personality made her many friends, and her yearbook reveals the sort of impression she left on the people at Stevens. The senior prediction was that she would become "a famous star of screen and radio."

In front of the Kelly family home, built by Jack, at 3901 Henry Avenue. Grace posed atop a jeep to be auctioned off at a benefit for the Stevens School, her alma mater, in 1953.

Be the pride of the neighborhood:

Philadelphia Main Line high society was a hard nut to crack, and the Kellys, whose wealth derived from bricklaying, were never accepted into this elite group. Even so, from the time she began making a name for herself in New York as a model, she had been and would remain Philadelphia's favorite daughter. It wasn't because her father was Jack Kelly, or because one of her uncles built the city's grand public library, or because her brother was an Olympic gold-medal winner. Grace made her city proud to call her its own for her own accomplishments. After moving to New York at the age of seventeen, Grace never again lived in Philadelphia, but she didn't forget her roots; she frequently returned to the City of Brotherly Love to spend time with her family.

Cotton candy for herself and for her niece at a summer festival for Women's Medical College, Philadelphia 1955.

Remember where you came from:

Over the years Grace stayed connected to the city of her birth in many ways. She brought the premiere of *To Catch a Thief* into town with Cary Grant in 1955; a year later she played out Philip Barry's famous play *The Philadelphia Story* in the screen musical adaptation, *High Society*; many local groups presented her with awards for her work in the arts over the years; and Grace was in town for the holidays of 1955–56, when she accepted a proposal of marriage from Prince Rainier. The couple formally announced their engagement at a luncheon held at the Philadelphia Country Club before some seventy reporters and photographers. When she was in town she also faithfully participated in charitable work and events for local organizations, always happy to use her celebrity for the benefit of her hometown.

Grace and Cary Grant get a kick out of the *Philadelphia Bulletin*'s report on their bringing the premiere of *To Catch a Thief* to her hometown.

"She was, and is, Philadelphia's once-and-always first lady."

—William Green, mayor of Philadelphia, 1980–84

CHAPTER TWO

Blonde Ambition:

How to Go
After Your Dreams

"I'm basically a feminist. I think that women can do anything they decide to do."

Looking sporty in stripes, with a penetrating Kelly gaze.

A successful model on the go in New York, 1949.

When people think about Grace, the image of the beautiful princess in a palace is what gets focused on, and so often her rise as an actress is glossed over. This is unfortunate because it is a terrific story of burning ambition and a lesson in resourcefulness, self-sufficiency, and old-fashioned perseverance.

Follow your dreams:

When Grace graduated from the Stevens School in 1947, her parents insisted that she go on to some form of higher education, so she set her sights on Bennington College in Vermont for its prestigious four-year dance program. She had been taking ballet lessons from the time she was a little girl and had performed on stage with the Philadelphia Old Academy Players from the age of eleven. At this point in her life, Grace's goal was to pursue a career in the performing arts. Her parents did not approve, but Grace's ambition had given her a determination and resolve that they had never before encountered in their daughter.

A young Grace gives her pitch for Old Gold cigarettes.

Sweater girl Grace, modeling (and drafting?) in 1948.

"I wanted to be a dancer, more than I wanted to be an actress. I tried to get into Bennington, because they had a great dance program there—Martha Graham was there, and other wonderful teachers. I was on the waiting list, but I didn't get in."

A pair of Grace's first modeling pictures.

"When I settled in New York . . . determined to become an actress, I didn't have any illusions as to how long it would take, and what I'd have to go through."

Use your connections . . . sparingly:

When Grace didn't make it into Bennington, she placed all her hopes in the American Academy of Dramatic Arts in New York and prepared to audition with a scene from her uncle's play *The Torchbearers*. George Kelly's niece was accepted. This was one instance in which she applied the use of name-dropping to help her career. With talent, ambition, a well-known uncle, and an old friend of her mother's to help arrange the audition, Grace entered the school where Edward G. Robinson, Spencer Tracy, Lauren Bacall, and Kirk Douglas had trained.

"We believe our children should have the right to choose their own careers. My wife and I try to advise and direct our children, but not stifle ambitions. When Grace insisted she would be an actress, we sent her to the American Academy of Dramatic Arts, secretly hoping, though, it was only a whim."

—Jack Kelly

An emerging star, 1953.

Be self-sufficient:

Grace moved into the Barbizon Hotel for Women on the Upper East Side. Her father paid her room and board at first, but she soon began taking modeling work in order to repay him.

After she finished her acting courses, modeling became Grace's mainstay. It was not how she wanted to earn a living, but at the age of nineteen it made her self-sufficient, and she was a natural. Her height may not have been ideal to fulfill her childhood dream of becoming a ballet dancer—once in heels it put her eye to eye with male co-stars on the stage—but her face and figure were perfect for the modeling world. By 1949 she was hopping between multiple assignments in a single day and earning $15 per hour, quite a handsome salary in those days.

"Every day I would leave the hotel in the morning, and I would be out until evening. If I didn't have a modeling job, I was looking for work in the theater, but nobody would hire me because they said I was too tall."

"Thanks to some lucky breaks in landing choice assignments in modeling jobs, I've been able to support myself fairly well. But I ride the subways like the rest of the girls, eat in drugstores, and yes, do my own laundry in the bathroom sink."

Cast your net wide:

Work on the Broadway stage was very difficult to land, but Grace did not give up. She was never a quitter. While she kept hoping she would eventually be hired for a role on Broadway, Grace took opportunities to play in summer stock, going on the road with companies of *The Torchbearers* and *The Heiress*. Back in New York between modeling assignments she pursued television work—both in dramatic roles and commercials. The medium was in its infancy. Everything about it was new and interesting, and the people working in the field learned as they went.

Broadway at last. Grace appears onstage with Raymond Massey as *The Father*.

"I worked in live television in the early '50s, and that was quite a challenge and very exciting. It was sort of the pioneer days of television, and it really was wonderful to be part of it."

Improve upon what nature gives you:

Upon her admittance to the Academy of Dramatic Arts, Grace's instructors noted that her voice was high and nasal. Determined to expel the unmistakable twang of a full-blooded Philadelphian from her vocal chords, Grace studied with voice coaches and listened to records until she achieved a unique Grace Kelly brand of perfect diction. Calling her voice "near British," as it is often described, doesn't capture it. It was all her own.

Be persistent:

Work in television and modeling was all well and good for the exposure and because it paid the bills, but the theater remained Grace's ultimate goal. In late 1949 she landed a legitimate role on Broadway. She had encountered so much opposition that by this time it was practically to her dismay that she was hired. Her role in August Strindberg's drama *The Father* was that of Bertha, with Raymond Massey and Mady Christians playing her parents.

"I've never been so nervous in all my life as when I showed up to read before Mr. Massey. I'm sure my hands shook as I held the manuscript. But

Grace as Ann Rutledge to Stephen Courtleigh's Abraham Lincoln on TV in 1950.

"We noticed that her voice was beginning to change. Instead of her old nasal whine, she was speaking in a lower, gentler register. Her sisters would make fun of her, but she would say, 'I must talk this way—for my work.'"

—Margaret Kelly

Publicity still for *High Noon*, with Katy Jurado, Gary Cooper, and Lloyd Bridges.

Mr. Massey was so kind and considerate. And later, the producers told me they wanted me back in two days to read before Mady Christians. . . . Right after the third reading, the stage manager of the show called me in my room and told me that I had the part and should report the following Tuesday for rehearsal!"

The play closed in January 1950. "[The show's closing] will mean I'll fall in line with the rest of my friends who are striving for parts. It means I go back to modeling, which has supported me these last two years—and even TV commercials. But anyone who wants to become an actress—a real actress—realizes it's all part of the game. You take the bits along with the big parts and keep hoping . . ."

Her exposure in the show, and racking up nearly a dozen TV miniseries credits, led to her being cast in her first feature film, *Fourteen Hours*. When asked about her first movie role, Grace said, "The critics couldn't see how [my character] had anything to do with the main plot." It was an inauspicious beginning to her film career, but a better opportunity was around the corner. With the help of her agent, Jay Kanter, Grace was chosen to star opposite Gary Cooper in *High Noon*.

On set as Amy Kane, in *High Noon*.

In full Quaker costume as the young bride, Amy Kane, in *High Noon*.

Don't wallow in self-doubt:

Beauty, brains, and talent didn't stop Grace from having doubts about herself early in her career. At the age of twenty-two, however, Grace had the energy of youth, was well-balanced in her outlook, and had the ability to recognize that it was not time to give up but time to work harder.

"I was terrible—honestly, anyone watching me give the pitch for Old Golds would have switched to Camels."

—On her TV commercials

"I've read for almost anything that's been cast. I even read for the ingénue part in *The Country Girl* on Broadway [left out in the movie]. The producer told me I really wasn't the ingénue type . . . "

—On trying to break into the theater

"In all my life, no one ever said, 'You are perfect.' People have been confused about my type, but they agreed on one thing: I was in the 'too' category— too tall, too leggy, too chinny."

—an early assessment from her New York days

With Gary Cooper
in *High Noon*.

"With Gary Cooper, everything is so clear. You look into his face, and see everything he is thinking. I looked into my own face, and saw nothing. I knew what I was thinking, but it didn't show. I suddenly thought, Perhaps I'm not going to be a great star. Perhaps I'm not any good after all."

—On *High Noon*

Go where the wind blows:

No one was overly impressed with her performance in *High Noon*, least of all Grace, but it led to the inevitable next step in her career—Hollywood.

"I didn't think I was ready. I thought I needed more training in the theater."

"I had to go to Hollywood because I couldn't get work on Broadway."

"We hoped she would give it up. Those movie people lead pretty shallow lives."

—Margaret Kelly

"I didn't want to be just another starlet."

Stopping in Philadelphia during a personal appearance tour for *High Noon*.

If you want something, speak up:

After *High Noon*, Grace was offered one of the lead roles in a big-budget production from MGM that was to be filmed in Africa. Grace said, "*Mogambo* had three things that interested me. John Ford, Clark Gable, and a trip to Africa with expenses paid. If *Mogambo* had been made in Arizona, I wouldn't have done it." There was one catch: in order to do *Mogambo*, Grace would have to sign a seven-year contract with the studio. Many actors would see this as a golden opportunity for steady work in films and an income while gaining experience. To Grace it meant servitude, as MGM would take complete control of her career and even her private life if she allowed them to. She wanted no part of it and had turned down studio offers in the past.

Ultimately, Grace's desire for an adventure in Africa outweighed her resistance to the studio system, but it would be on her terms. She agreed to sign with MGM only after the studio agreed to her concessions, including time off between films to do plays.

Ava Gardner, Clark Gable, and Grace, back from Africa and on a studio set, making high heels on safari possible again.

Be adventurous:

After ironing out the terms with the studio, Grace headed to Africa to work on *Mogambo* with Clark Gable and Ava Gardner—and it was indeed an adventure. There was always the threat of being attacked by wandering wild animals in the filming area, so cast and crew were all issued guns to protect themselves should the need arise. There were three deaths from auto accidents, and many members of the company became ill from tropical infections. Meanwhile, Grace fell into a romance with the handsome Gable during filming. She returned with a glowing review of Africa.

In Africa, Grace and Gable get friendly with members of a local tribe.

In Africa with Clark Gable for *Mogambo*

"I have always been fascinated by Africa. . . .

And believe me, I have not been disappointed."

On location in Afri… with Clark Gable as Actor … A…littl…

Always do your best— you never know who's watching:

Grace earned an Academy Award nomination as Best Supporting Actress for her performance in *Mogambo*, though, truth be told, the film does not hold up well under modern scrutiny with its high melodrama and depiction of relations between "Great White Hunters" and African natives. In 1953, though, the movie made her one of the most sought-after actresses in town. At this point one of the most influential men in Grace's life entered the scene—Alfred Hitchcock.

Fire and Ice:

Achieving That Mysterious Air

*"I'm not an extrovert, but I'm not unfriendly either.
I'm not the exuberant type, but I don't like
to read that I'm cold and distant. I don't think I am."*

$\mathcal{A}$*fter watching a test she had made* at Fox for the film *Taxi*, "Master of Suspense" director Alfred Hitchcock wanted Grace to star in his next film, *Dial M for Murder*. He saw Grace as the personification of his ideal actress—a woman who embodied the "Fire and Ice" paradox, a cool, untouchable quality on the surface, simmering with sensuality and a dynamic personality just beneath.

Grace listens intently to director Alfred Hitchcock on the set of their first film together.

Play the murder scene like a love scene, was Grace's directive from Hitchcock.

"Mr. Hitchcock taught me everything about cinema. It was thanks to him that I understood that murder scenes should be shot like love scenes and love scenes like murder scenes."

As Margot Wendice, *Dial M for Murder*.

"From the *Taxi* test, you could see Grace's potential for restraint. I always tell actors: Don't use the face for nothing. Don't start scribbling over the sheet of paper until we have something to write. We may need it later. Grace has this control. It's a rare thing for a girl at such an age."

—Alfred Hitchcock

Portrait of an MGM star.

"I could not think of anything to say to him. In a horrible way it seemed funny to have my brain turned to stone."

—On meeting Alfred Hitchcock

"She's an emotional actress, and in spite of her cool, calm exterior, she does have feelings. In many ways I think she is perhaps more emotional than most people."

—Margaret Kelly

The character of Tracy Lord in *High Society* played on Grace's cool persona.

"Maybe she has fire and ice and great passion, but she does not flaunt it."

—Alfred Hitchcock

"I'm a cold goddess," Grace as Tracy Lord in *High Society*.

Sending a model of the yacht *True Love* on its maiden voyage across the family pool in *High Society*.

"When you look at Grace, she reminds you of a cool breeze of fresh air."

—Bing Crosby

One of her last MGM portrait sittings, 1956.

Define yourself and be consistent:

Hollywood stars, particularly in the classic era, had distinctive screen personas that couldn't help but be infused with large amounts of the performer's true character. A megastar's megawatt personality always shines through in a performance, and it is that truth that an audience embraces. In the case of Grace Kelly, what a wonderful treat it is to see her personality light up the screen. Perhaps no character embodies Grace Kelly like Lisa Fremont in *Rear Window*.

After starring in *Dial M for Murder*, Grace was "it." For her next film she had a choice between working with director Elia Kazan on his gritty drama about longshoremen *On the Waterfront*, or staying on with Hitchcock for *Rear Window*, which came complete with an Edith Head wardrobe, co-star James Stewart, and the glow of Technicolor. The choice was clear. Grace reached for a set of binoculars and slipped into Lisa Fremont's silk nightgown and organdy dresses. Eva Marie Saint took the part of Edie Doyle opposite Marlon Brando in *On the Waterfront*.

Grace was not always a risk taker when it came to her career. Playing Lisa Fremont was no stretch for her, but by no means was it a bad move. It wasn't

Lisa Fremont, a girl who never wears the same dress twice.

When James Stewart awakes from a nap to this vision, we are uncertain for a moment whether she is a dream or reality.

Grace and Thelma Ritter handle James Stewart's legwork in *Rear Window*.

that she was afraid to take a chance, it's just that she knew how to choose her battles. And she could sense which was the better opportunity for her at the time. From the moment her face entered the frame in a dreamlike entrance twenty minutes into the film, Grace was clearly fixed as a goddess and a superstar in the Hollywood pantheon.

If Lisa Fremont represents the quintessential Grace Kelly role, there are many life lessons to be learned from this screen alter ego.

Make an entrance

Few entrances in films can compare to the close-up and kiss between Grace and James Stewart in her opening moments in *Rear Window*. Grace said, "They certainly ought to be the closest love scenes of all time. The camera has been inches away from our faces. The other day I asked if my hair needed fixing. Hitch told me my hair wasn't in the picture; just my face. Can you imagine how it will look on the wide screen?" Breathtaking is the word.

Spoil those you love . . . once in a while

Lisa knows that her normally active boyfriend, Jeff, is miserable being cloistered in his apartment while nursing a broken leg. She promises to make it a week he'll never forget. Starting by surprising him with a bottle of wine and his favorite meal, she proves to be a woman of her word.

Beware of seeming too perfect

Lisa can't help being perceived as "too perfect" by Jeff, a quality he finds somewhat intimidating. But if he didn't deserve the best from her, a woman like Lisa would not waste time on him.

Be his partner in crime

Skeptical about his suspicions at first, Lisa soon becomes just as enthralled as Jeff in the questionable activity he observes. And she takes seriously her role as his partner in unraveling the mystery. Temporarily bound to his wheelchair, Lisa becomes his "legs" and shows fearlessness in scaling walls to gain entry to the home of a cold-blooded killer.

Grace as Lisa Fremont, a perfect partner in crime(solving), sitting on James Stewart's rear window ledge.

James Stewart has Grace autograph a miniature of the leg cast of L. B. Jeffries.

Be a lady—and one of the boys

Lisa is intelligent and as high class a lady as they come, but she is also playful and shows an irresistible tomboyish streak.

Dress impeccably

White gloves? Check. Pearls? Check. Color coordinated? Check.

Be disarming:

The character of Francie Stevens in *To Catch a Thief* is the cinematic sister of Lisa Fremont. They have much in common, most importantly that Hitchockian essential—the intangible quality of fire and ice. Removed from the confines of a one-room set to the French Riviera, Francie has new circumstances under which to disarm her audience with unexpected passion and a lust for life. She also presents us with her own lessons to live by.

Cast and crew celebrate Alfred Hitchcock's birthday on the set of *To Catch a Thief*, April 1954.

How to catch a thief? Take him by surprise.

Don't be afraid to make the first move

Nothing is sexier to a man when the chemistry's there.

Be a head turner

But never acknowledge the attention, of course.

If you must flirt, do it with a well-placed double entendre

But use with caution; nobody could put over a *double entendre* like Grace Kelly.
She could make a risqué subtext sound ladylike.

Framed in a doorway as Francie Stevens.

A bottle of suntan oil in hand, Francie Stevens lounges seaside.

Don't get rattled by the competition

Just put on one of your best evening gowns and make your man forget all about her.

Find a great setting

A glorious backdrop could never compete with you; it only serves as a glorious picture frame.

Make a statement with accessories

That magnificent diamond necklace she wears served a two-fold purpose. It enticed Cary Grant and was the perfect adornment to a gorgeous white strapless gown.

Display beauty and brains

A man worth having would never be intimidated by intelligence, so don't be afraid to show it.

Francie believes her jewels are the way to catch this thief, but she has plenty of her own allure.

If you're wrong, be the first to admit it, as graciously as Francie does.

Let life imitate art:

Lisa Fremont and Francie Stevens are the paradigms of what we can learn from Grace Kelly's screen persona, which to an extent was reflective of the woman herself, but there are a few nuggets of wisdom to be gleaned from other characters that Grace brought to life, even if they weren't of the "fire and ice" variety.

Stand by your man

Amy Kane of *High Noon* threatens to leave her new husband soon after their marriage, but she just never gets around to making her exit. When push comes to shove and a posse of criminals descends upon Will Kane, Amy can't go along with the rest of the town and desert the man she loves.

Gary Cooper as Marshal Will Kane, Grace his Quaker wife, Amy, in *High Noon*.

Ava Gardner, Clark Gable, and Grace, depicting the love triangle of *Mogambo*.

As Linda Nordley, Grace played the damsel in distress to the hilt.

Certain men just love "helpless" women

Her character of Linda Nordley in *Mogambo* was not cut from the same mold as the earthy creature played by co-star Ava Gardner. In the African brush Linda proved that men just love to help a so-called "damsel in distress." Of course you know you're self-sufficient but there's no shame in accepting a helping hand now and then, especially when you know the tables can turn at any moment.

At Paramount
while filming
The Country Girl.

Stick it out through thick and thin

In her marriage to the alcoholic Frank Elgin, Georgie (*The Country Girl*) knew the full meaning of the marriage vow that called her to remain steadfast "for better or for worse." The "worse" hardened her personality and dulled her looks. She is world-weary far beyond her years, but with tough love she pulls her husband through his lowest moments with her own spirit intact and stronger than ever. William Holden's character is taken with her, saying, "You're impertinent . . . and you're loyal, steadfast, and devoted. I like that in a woman."

Beware of wolves in sheep's clothing

Dial M for Murder's Margot Wendice is blissfully unaware that her husband knows all about the affair she is having and is plotting to murder her.

Remember that nobody loves a statue

Princess Alexandra in *The Swan* was something of a caricature of Grace's cool persona, stripped of the spirit of Grace's society-girl roles. Alexandra is a girl of unseen depths, however, and after spending time with her brothers' handsome tutor she no longer requires a shot of spirits to cultivate her *joie de vivre*.

Grace the princess and Louis Jourdan the tutor in *The Swan*.

Let your tiara slip a little

Another "swan" and ice queen who needed help off her pedestal was Tracy

Lord in *High Society*. Only then could Tracy find happiness.

Fencing on the set of *The Swan*.

Go out with a bang

High Society was the last feature film in which Grace starred, though she wasn't certain it would turn out that way at the time. Co-starring Frank Sinatra, Bing Crosby, Louis Armstrong, and Celeste Holm, it was a beautiful end to her Hollywood career. It was also Grace's first musical, and she decided to go whole hog and contribute to the soundtrack. With its haunting melody and lyrics by Cole Porter, "True Love" was a worthy swan song for the actress who was about to walk away from her acting career for, well, true love. The song was a hit and made Grace a platinum recording artist.

The stars of *High Society*—Bing Crosby, Grace, Frank Sinatra, and Celeste Holm.

A candid shot from the set of *High Society*.

CHAPTER FOUR

Work Ethics:

Making It
a Job Well Done

"Acting is a very time-consuming profession to do well."

More than a beautiful face,
Grace was a consummate professional.

Arguably, Grace's greatest professional risk, her greatest fight for a role, and the one that reaped the greatest reward, was playing Georgie Elgin in *The Country Girl*. Grace pulled her hair back into an unflattering bun, wiped off most of her makeup, and donned a pair of spectacles. The nearsighted Grace very much needed glasses, but she rarely wore them in her private life, let alone on the big screen. Her stellar performance won her the most coveted prize among actresses, the Academy Award for Best Actress.

"If I can't do this picture, I'll get on the train and never come back. I'll quit the picture business."

"I was very anxious to play such a wonderful part, but I was very nervous at the beginning. . . . Paramount went on a limb to borrow me from MGM and I kept worrying, what if I disappoint them?

Dressed down and bespectacled, Grace gladly left the glamour behind for *The Country Girl*.

Accept accolades graciously:

Grace accepted her Oscar for *The Country Girl* with typical poise, modesty, and warmth. She appeared genuinely thrilled and grateful to those who worked with her on the film.

"The thrill of this moment keeps me from saying how I really feel. I can only say thank you with all my heart to all who made this possible for me. Thank you."

"You never know how exciting it can be until it happens to you."

"For me it was a wonderful moment, one I shall cherish sincerely forever. I am overwhelmed and grateful. I'm a very lucky girl."

"The girl who wins this part wins the Oscar."

—Producer William Perlberg's "note to self"

With upswept hair and pearls, Grace's Georgie Elgin gains subtle glamour by the end of *The Country Girl*.

Accompanied by Paramount executive Don Hartman at the Academy Awards.

At the Oscars with presenter William Holden.

At the Oscars in 1955, most thought Judy Garland in *A Star is Born*, not Grace, would win. Judy herself took the loss hard. "I really thought Judy would win it," said Grace.

Bob Hope, Master of Ceremonies at the Academy Awards in 1955, plants a kiss on the year's Best Actress.

With pearl-drop earrings and floral hair adornments, a trace of apprehension shows on the face of Oscar nominee Grace.

Cutting a celebratory cake in honor of her Oscar win.

Be pragmatic:

Grace was ecstatic about the win, of course, but was also realistic about the transient quality of fame.

"Next year, it will be somebody else. . . . I'm delighted it's me right now."

"Having won the Oscar puts you in a wonderful position. You get a better choice of roles. But it does put you up for more criticism. You're judged more severely. The important thing to do is to just keep working."

Work well with others:

Grace was well known for her professionalism among the cast and crew of her films. She had an amazing memory and learning lines came easily to her. She always got along well with the people behind the scenes, including a wardrobe woman who was interviewed for her thoughts on Grace on the set of one of her movies: "She's so nice she doesn't seem like other actresses. By that I mean that she's undemanding. Most movie actresses get so accustomed to having things done for them—their hair combed, a chair reserved, a wrap delivered— that they expect people to jump at their slightest desire. Not Grace Kelly. She never asks anyone to do anything she can do for herself."

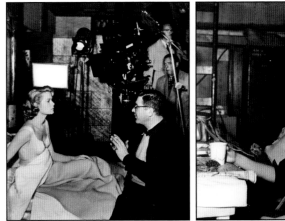

Preparing for a scene in *The Bridges at Toko-Ri*.

Crew members adored Grace.

On the set with William Holden.

"With some actresses, you have to keep snapping them to attention like a puppy. Grace is always concentrating. In fact, she sometimes keeps me on the track."

—William Holden

Grace tended to display her left side for photos, but her face photographed beautifully from any angle.

Experimenting with an exotic look. She was a great subject and photographers and makeup artists enjoyed trying different things out with her.

"She's easy to play to. You can see her thinking the way she's supposed to think in the role. You know she's listening, and not just for cues. Some actresses don't think and don't listen. You can tell they're just counting the words."

—James Stewart

"She'll be different in every movie she makes. Not because of makeup or clothes but because she plays a character from the inside out. There's no one else like her in Hollywood."

—Alfred Hitchcock

"Grace doesn't throw everything at you in the first five seconds. Some girls give you everything they've got at once, and there it is—there is no more. But Grace is like a kaleidoscope: one twist, and you get a whole new facet."

—George Seaton, director of *The Country Girl*

"[After only two takes] I understood the envy some Hollywood stars have of her—the girl is an artist, and recognizably one in a city brimful of talent."

—Alec Guinness

Take the good with the bad:

With so many hours spent at work every day, having to face a job you dislike can be detrimental to both your physical and spiritual well-being. Grace refused to follow any of the conventional career routes for women of her day because at a young age she felt with all her being that she wanted to devote her time and talent to acting. She came to realize there were difficulties for her to accept, however, even in the profession that she loved.

"An actress creates what she wants but she has no sense of balance. Oh how can I express it? I know what I'm doing in a film but I cannot be objective. The director sees all facets and balances one against the other. He controls what he gets."

Stepping out of her dressing room ready to film *High Society*.

Candid shot of Grace at the studio.

"I loved acting. I loved working in the theater and pictures. I didn't particularly like being a movie star. There's a big difference."

"I had no illusions when I selected the stage as a career. I was completely aware of the grueling apprenticeship and the constant practice necessary to put the fine, artistic polish on portrayal of character."

Choose your battles:

Grace was at the peak of her career after winning the Oscar for *The Country Girl.* She was officially an MGM actress, but thus far had made only one film for the studio since the start of her contract. Grace's agency, MCA, with Jay Kantor as her representative, had done a terrific job securing consecutive loan-outs by MGM for Grace's services to other studios. The movies she made

Signing on the dotted line? This was a photo session for a series run in a magazine in 1954, not actual MGM deal-making.

Lunching with cast and crew in Colombia during the filming of *Green Fire* in 1954.

at Warner Bros. and Paramount, *The Country Girl* and the Hitchcock films, were ones she wanted to do very much. What MGM was offering didn't interest her. The specialties of the studio were costume films and musicals, neither of which was particularly well suited to Grace. When she turned down one too many roles, MGM put her on suspension.

"I don't want to dress up a picture with just my face," Grace said. That is precisely what she did when she finally accepted one of the roles MGM was offering in the spring of 1954. The film was *Green Fire*. At least it allowed Grace to visit another foreign country—Colombia.

On location in Colombia for the filming of *Green Fire*.

Stewart Granger, Grace, and a horse prepare for a scene in *Green Fire*.

The lighting crew sets up a scene for *Green Fire*, with Grace and Stewart Granger.

With co-star Paul Douglas in Colombia during the making of *Green Fire*.

Next she was reunited with Hitchcock for their third and final film together. *To Catch a Thief* put Grace back in the glamour-girl mold of *Rear Window*, enhanced to the nth degree with the French Riviera as her backdrop. Grace's popularity soared after its release. In 1955 she ranked number two in exhibitors' national polls, just below James Stewart and above John Wayne, with her co-stars William Holden and Gary Cooper rounding out the top five.

As for Grace, the studio walls began to close in on her. With *To Catch a Thief*, she had been away from MGM for yet another film. The studio did indeed profit from the loan-outs, but now knew that the greater profit was in having her in their own productions. But unlike most actresses, Grace was not satisfied to simply be employed by a studio, and she wasn't afraid to fight her bosses if she didn't feel a part was right for her. She had turned down *Jeremy Rodock*, in spite of the fact that Spencer Tracy was to be her co-star, saying it was "a wonderful script, and an honor to be given the chance to play opposite Mr. Tracy. [But the role] is not for me." The title of *Jeremy Rodock* was later changed to *Tribute to a Bad Man*, starring James Cagney—the meaty role in the film was not for a woman.

She also refused *The Cobweb*, in which she was replaced by Lauren Bacall and then *Quentin Durward*, which went to Kay Kendall. Another film she declined, the 1957 version of *The Barretts of Wimpole Street*, was eventually cast with Jennifer Jones.

Grace waits for her turn before the cameras.

"I felt I had to turn down the roles; they're just parts I couldn't see myself playing."

"MGM wants me to do *The Barretts of Wimpole Street*, but I'm too young. I don't want to seem temperamental, and there are several other roles at MGM I would be delighted to accept. But they don't seem to agree with me about those."

"All I'd do would be to wear thirty-five different costumes, look pretty and frightened. . . . I just thought I'd be so bored."

—on typical MGM roles she was offered

CHAPTER FIVE

Gentlemen Prefer Ladies:

How to Be a Style Icon

"She wanted to be remembered as a lady.
And that's precisely what she was."

—Howell Conant

In Hollywood, beauties were and continue to be a dime a dozen, but a beautiful actress whom both the press and the public can sense is a genuine lady is a rare commodity. In the era of Gina Lollobrigida, Marilyn Monroe, Jayne Mansfield, and the other buxom-blonde Monroe imitators, Grace and another contemporary, Audrey Hepburn, stood apart. Grace didn't alienate female audiences in the way that a sexy "bombshell" type could; she was a woman other women wished to be. She was also the woman every man would like to marry. When *Time* magazine ran a cover story on Grace in 1955, the headline "Gentlemen Prefer Ladies" modified the title of Anita Loos's famous novel to fit the style of this particular blonde.

"The only time she gives me any trouble is when the proofs are ready. She kills all shots that show too much leg, too much cleavage, or soulful, sexy eyes."

—Bud Fraker, Paramount photographer

The fresh-faced all-American girl of the '50s.

At the
1956 Oscars.

Dressed to the nines for her final big Hollywood event, the Academy Awards in 1956.

"Nobody came to see me before wearing white gloves."

—*High Noon* director Fred Zinneman's first reaction to Grace

Alfred Hitchcock, Grace, and James Stewart at the premiere of *Rear Window*.

Be inspirational:

In her Hollywood years she was a muse for the top studio designers. Edith Head worked with her at Paramount. At MGM she inspired Helen Rose, who even came up with a film about a fashion designer, *Designing Woman*,

Preparing for a portrait sitting.

"She has a great eye and great style; you know she will wear anything beautifully."

—Helen Rose

in which Grace was supposed to star before her marriage to Prince Rainier in 1956. It turned out that Lauren Bacall got the part and Grace got the prince. Helen Rose then came up with the most famous gown of Grace Kelly's life— the one in which she was wed.

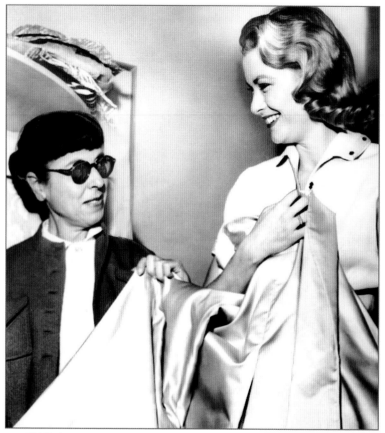

Edith Head shows Grace the coat she will wear over her blue satin gown at the Academy Awards.

Showing off every glorious fold of her costume ball gown, an Edith Head design, on the set of *To Catch a Thief*.

"She selects clothes and stories and directors with the same sureness. It's fantastic. She's always right."

—Edith Head

Grace carries the famous Hermès "Kelly Bag."

Find signature pieces:

Grace had an instinct for fashion. More importantly, she knew what looked good on her. Her signature accessories are hallmarks of a classy lady today. She wore pearl necklaces, usually a single-strand choker; white gloves of every length; large sunglasses; and hats that complemented her attire rather than competed with it. In 1956 Grace began to be seen toting a structured Hermès crocodile handbag at all times. The "Kelly Bag," named after the woman who made it famous, has been a staple among fashionable women for decades.

Grace's passion for gloves was inherited from her mother, seated at right.

Mother and daughter attend Easter Sunday services at St. Bridget's Church in Philadelphia, 1956. Margaret Kelly influenced Grace's fashion sensibility.

"[Our] mother was a stickler for dressing appropriately for the occasion. I am sure Mother's influence was in some way responsible for Grace's white gloves—and hats."

—Lizanne Kelly

Travel attire—scarf, sunglasses, gloves, poodle—Grace arrives in New York with fellow actresses Elizabeth Taylor and Laraine Day, 1954.

Keep a sense of balance:

Grace's casual wear still holds up. She wore flats, Capri pants, jeans, and classic menswear button-down shirts. Her style was sophisticated and yet unpretentious at the same time. It seemed to say "less is more." The fact that Grace didn't take her role as a style icon too seriously was part of her appeal. In the mid-1950s, as she began winning fashion awards and being named to "Best-Dressed" lists, she couldn't understand what the fuss was all about.

"I don't think I'm *that* different. I sometimes think they talk about [my style] because there's not much happening to me."

"Grace wanted to be considered serious. A consuming interest in apparel was not, in her eyes, the hallmark of a serious person."

—Oleg Cassini

Casual in slacks, 1954.

"By wearing clothes that don't get too much notice, she gets noticed more herself."

—Oleg Cassini

Pairing a classic menswear white shirt with a classic tweed skirt.

Taking a turn around the MGM lot, 1954.

Relaxing in style.

Grace loved to use scarves for fashion in many ways, including around her head, tied to a belt loop, or around her neck.

Be frugal:

Before buying new clothes, Grace had to feel they would hold up well for years—she simply never threw things away. Grace's understated way also manifested itself in the fact that she was famously frugal. Fashion accessories were the only items on which she was known to splurge—occasionally. For instance, she treated herself upon completion of *High Noon*: "As soon as the picture was finished, I went right out and bought myself a mink stole. It was something I'd wanted, but couldn't afford before."

"I just buy clothes when they take my eyes, and I wear them for years."

Making a statement with jewelry, 1955.

A vision in white Christian Dior.

Displaying one of the intricate hairdos with which Grace liked to experiment.

"If there is one
thing that is
foreign to me
it is shopping
for pleasure."

Looking every inch a queen with tiara and diamond-and-ruby necklace in
Monaco, 1956.

Grace's wardrobe from *High Society* became part of her trousseau, a wedding gift from MGM.

Trying on a contribution from hat designer John Fredericks to her wedding trousseau.

"[Grace] couldn't drop something just because it went out of fashion, she was very sentimental about her clothes."

Grace arrives with Oleg Cassini at a movie premiere, 1954.

"Gloves and shoes are the only things where Grace loses count of money."

—Edith Head

Keep fit:

Grace presented the very picture of health. Impeccably well groomed, her complexion showed vitality and her golden hair shone. She was all-American and freshly scrubbed—"the girl next door."

Grace was 5'6½" but her poise and carriage made her seem taller. She wore a size ten in the '50s, which today would be about the equivalent of a size four. It was the smallest available "off the rack" then. Grace had a healthy appetite. She loved to eat, especially pasta, and had to restrain herself at the table to maintain her slim figure even in her twenties. She would forego the doughnuts placed at her disposal by the studio and start her day with a small bowl of oatmeal for breakfast, then she would fight hunger on the set by nibbling on carrots, celery, dried fruit, and graham crackers. Later in life it became a greater struggle for her, and at those times reporters were ever ready to record her fluctuations in weight.

Making a statement in casual wear, *To Catch a Thief*.

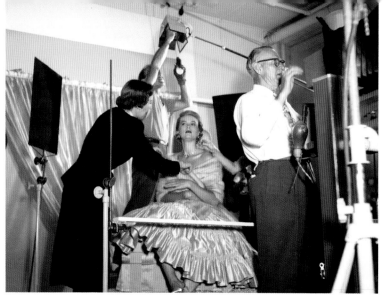

A multitude of hands prepare a Grace Kelly photo session.

Trust your instincts:

Wearing a nightgown in the murder scene in *Dial M for Murder* was Grace's idea, perhaps to some degree influenced by the fact that Hitchcock had given her the directive to play it like a love scene. The director wanted her to wear a robe, but Grace argued that if she had been woken suddenly in the night she wouldn't bother to put on a robe to answer the telephone.

"After this I had his confidence as far as wardrobe was concerned. He gave me a great deal of liberty in what I would wear in the next two pictures for him, and when he brought in Edith Head to design the clothes, she and I worked together wonderfully well."

Wear it well:

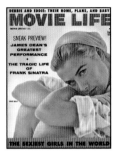

Grace had been one of the top models in New York in the late 1940s and had learned from experience how to make a garment photograph well. This knowledge came in handy in Hollywood. Edith Head witnessed it firsthand on the set of their first film together, while at the same time getting a lesson on how to deal with a strong male personality:

"At the rehearsal for the scene in *Rear Window* when I wore a sheer nightgown, Hitchcock called for Edith Head. He came over here and said, 'Look, the bosom is not right, we're going to have to put something in there.' He was very sweet about it; he didn't want to upset me, so he spoke quietly to Edith.

"We went into my dressing room, and Edith said, 'Mr. Hitchcock is worried because there's a false pleat here. He wants me to put in falsies.' Well, I said, 'You can't put falsies in this, it's going to show and I'm not going to wear them.' And she said, 'What are we going to do?' So we quickly took it up here, made some adjustments there, and I just did what I could and stood as straight as possible—without falsies. When I walked out onto the set Hitchcock looked at me and at Edith and said, 'See what a difference they make?'"

CHAPTER SIX

Friends and Lovers:

Maintaining Lasting Relationships

"She was a great lady, and also great fun ..."

—Ava Gardner

Grace was great at making and maintaining relationships with the people she encountered at various stages of her life. She hated to fight and had an easygoing attitude that never allowed her to remain angry with those she cared about for very long. Her cool image may have been intimidating to some, but the durability of her relationships proves that Grace was indeed approachable and that her charm and personality made people want to remain in her company as long as they could.

Remember birthdays:

Ava Gardner was Grace's co-star in *Mogambo*, and the two remained friends ever after. Ava later wrote about how touched she was that Grace never forgot her birthday. Without fail, a gift of some sort would turn up for her on her special day, along with a personal note written in Grace's hand. Ava, Frank Sinatra, James Stewart, David Niven, Elizabeth Taylor, Lauren Bacall, Cary Grant, and Alfred Hitchcock were among Grace's lifelong friends from the Hollywood days.

Sharing a laugh with *High Society* co-stars Bing Crosby, Celeste Holm, and Frank Sinatra.

Grace and Louis Armstrong got along famously while making *High Society*.

With longtime friend David Niven, Grace was comfortable wearing her oh-so-necessary but oh-so-seldom-worn glasses.

Keep in touch:

As noted by Ava Gardner, Grace was well-known for keeping up correspondence with those she cared about. Grace was far removed from most of these people, so from a note to a former co-star on her birthday to a message of congratulations to her brother to a thank-you message for a gift received, Grace's personal notes were a mark of her loyalty and thoughtfulness and the secret to her lifelong relationships.

With no hint of romance, Grace and co-star James Stewart became great friends.

"All my friends go back a long time,
further back than Hollywood."

Be hospitable:

There were many aspects of Hollywood that Grace despised from day one, such as the weather, the gossip-mongers, and the way MGM tried to manage her career. But after leaving, she missed the town's social life and her friends. Anytime a Hollywood luminary was in Monaco, he or she was welcomed with open arms. Grace's hospitality was well known and any friend or family member had an open invitation to the palace.

Be yourself:

Grace called this the best way to "win friends and take laurels in the poise and popularity field."

Grace and co-star Cary Grant at the premiere of *To Catch a Thief*, Philadelphia 1955.

Be there for your friends:

Though she had endless obligations to fulfill, Grace was often at Alfred Hitchcock's side at events celebrating the director's work. She also faithfully made her way back to Philadelphia for events such as weddings in the Kelly family.

Lend a hand:

Largely rejected by America and embraced by Europe, the African-American dancer, singer, and actress Josephine Baker had been one of the great entertainers on the Continent during the 1920s. The big-hearted Josephine wanted to make a home for orphans from all parts of the world. Unfortunately, she wanted to take care of them all herself, in her own home, and ran up insurmountable debts that resulted in her family being evicted from their chateau in France. Grace stepped in and offered Josephine and her "Rainbow Tribe," as the orphans were called, a home in Monaco. When Baker passed away in 1975, Grace handled the funeral arrangements as well.

Grace was on hand to celebrate Alfred Hitchcock at Lincoln Center in 1974.

Love and learn:

It is no surprise that men fell at the feet of Grace Kelly from the time she was a teenager. Possessing looks, personality, talent, heart, and a gentle quality that made men want to take care of her, she was irresistible. Grace was a romantic soul, and having the pick of the most handsome and personable men in Philadelphia, New York, and Hollywood, she naturally fell into her fair share of romances.

On a film set, where wildly attractive people are asked to pretend to be in love, the line between fantasy and reality is apt to blur. Grace was romantically linked to actors Gary Cooper, Clark Gable, Ray Milland, Jean-Pierre Aumont, Bing Crosby, and William Holden, a lineup that shocked some in the '50s and raises eyebrows even today as the love life of Grace Kelly continues to be a topic of interest. Oftentimes affairs between co-stars could be kept secret from the public. Grace's string of romantic attachments became known in large part because Margaret Kelly, of all people, wrote a series of articles on her daughter's life, containing a detailed chronology of her boyfriends. The stories were published shortly before Grace's marriage to Prince Rainier.

Grace and William Holden, husband and wife in *The Bridges at Toko-Ri*.

Grace and William Holden.

"Her quietness made everyone feel that they ought to take care of her. . . . She must have struck men the same way she struck me. Every man who knew her from the time she was about fifteen and even before that wanted to take care of Gracie. . . . Our house was everlastingly full of mooning boys."

—Margaret Kelly

Holden sees active combat in *The Bridges at Toko-Ri*, separating him from his wife.

Don't be a gossip:

During the early '50s Grace was swiftly becoming a star of the first order. In a town as competitive as Hollywood, it was not difficult to breed jealousy on the way to the top. Grace was branded in some quarters as a brazen, ambitious starlet, particularly among women in town who attempted to cast her in a negative light. It was unfair to suggest that she was attempting to advance her career in any way; with Grace romance was sparked by her intensely romantic nature, a charming male personality, and mutual attraction, not ambition.

"As an unmarried woman, I was thought to be a danger. Other women looked at me as a rival and it pained me a great deal. . . . The persecution didn't last long; I had a circle of good friends. But even so, I hated Hollywood. It's a town without pity."

"Hollywood amuses me. Holier-than-thou for the public and unholier-than-the-devil in reality."

Make him
come to you:

Fashion designer Oleg Cassini was a big romance in Grace's life. He had been married to actress Gene Tierney, whom Richard Widmark called "an early Grace Kelly." Like Grace, Tierney was from a prominent East Coast family, came to Hollywood by way of the New York theater scene, and possessed cultured style and rare beauty. Oleg had become fascinated with Grace upon seeing her in *Mogambo* and set out to woo and win this woman by anonymously sending flowers to her—every day. By the time her flower sender's identity was revealed, she was intrigued enough to go on a date with him—with her sister Peggy along as chaperone.

According to Oleg, when Grace went to France to film *To Catch a Thief*, she sent him a note reading, "Those who love me, follow me." He promptly followed, and they spent a lovely vacation together during which they became engaged. Grace's family disapproved of Cassini, largely because he was a twice-divorced man and because he was not Catholic. In this instance, Grace was truly charmed by Oleg's undeniable charm and basked in the glow of his devotion—but his love for her was greater than hers for him.

Out on the town with Oleg Cassini, New York 1955.

"Do you realize if my mother hadn't been so difficult about Oleg Cassini I probably would have married him?"

—Grace, uncharacteristically frank with an inquisitive reporter

Be a sport:

When Grace was given the opportunity to star in *Mogambo*, she was thrilled at the thought of filming in Africa, but also at the thought of working with Clark Gable, the "King of Hollywood." Gable loved blondes, and Grace certainly had his attention for a time. Roughing it with him in Africa must have reminded him of his sporting first wife, Carole Lombard, whom friends say he never got over after her tragic death in a plane crash in 1942.

Clark Gable sees Grace off to America upon completion of *Mogambo*.

"Gracie was a good Catholic girl, and she was having a hard time feeling the way she did about Clark."

—Ava Gardner, *Mogambo* co-star

Grace and Gable at the Academy Awards, 1954.

"Grace had more of a schoolgirl crush on Gable than any-thing else. After all, it was thrilling for her to be with a man who had been at the top of his profession for so many years. Any young girl would have been thrilled."

—Margaret Kelly

Discover what you want in a life partner:

Clearly Grace loved the notion of being in love. She enjoyed time with men of appealing looks and character, but it took experience for her to learn that these traits alone were not what she wanted in a husband. Both in her personal and professional life, Grace tended to be most devoted to strong men with dominant personalities. The man she married would also have to share her values and preferably be Catholic. He must impress the Kelly family as well; even if she didn't always agree with them, their approval remained of the utmost importance to Grace. She also wanted a man who would not be overshadowed by her. When asked what she looked for in a husband, one consistent answer was, "I don't want to be married to someone who feels inferior to my success."

Actor Jean-Pierre Aumont was Grace's constant companion in Cannes in 1955. "Don't worry, I have lost neither my heart nor mind," said Grace via telegram to her family regarding Aumont.

170

Jean-Pierre Aumont says goodbye to Grace. She was going home to America following the Cannes Film Festival.

"I needed someone with a strong personality to hold his own against the fame of an actress. I have never wanted to marry a man who would have allowed himself to become Mister Kelly."

CHAPTER SEVEN

To Catch a Prince:

Finding "The One"

"I like girls who look natural.
And I will not remain a bachelor all my life."

—**Prince Rainier**

Rainier and Grace share the last dance
at their engagement party, 1956.

As ambitious as Grace was to succeed in her career as an actress, her romantic soul would never have allowed her to be content with success alone. Someday, she knew, she would find the love of her life and have children with him. In May 1955, Grace was in the south of France for the Cannes Film Festival. En route she had met Pierre Galante, an editor for *Paris Match*, a popular magazine that was looking for a very special story—a meeting between a real-life prince and a reel-life movie queen. Would she be willing to meet Prince Rainier Grimaldi?

The history of the Grimaldi dynasty dates back seven hundred years, longer than any other ruling family or sovereign government in Europe. Monaco, bordered on three sides by France and situated along the Mediterranean, was officially recognized as a principality, or independent sovereign state, by the Franco-Monegasque Treaty of 1861. By the 1950s, the principality was most famous for its Grand Casino of Monte Carlo, its Grand Prix, and its lack of taxation upon its citizens. Rainier Louis Henri Maxence Bertrand Grimaldi ascended to his role of Sovereign Prince of Monaco in November 1949. Like Oleg Cassini and Jean-Pierre Aumont, he was a continental type who intrigued Grace, but when she agreed to the photo shoot with him proposed by Pierre Galante, it seemed of no great importance. Prince

A movie star waves to fans at the Cannes Film Festival in 1955.

The pattern of the dress Grace wore when she met Prince Rainier was printed and made available to millions of aspiring princesses around the world.

Rainier could not have qualified as a fan of Grace Kelly the actress either. He had reportedly only seen her in *Green Fire*, not one of her finest credits.

On the day of her meeting with the prince at his palace, Grace was running late, but when she arrived she found that he was running even later. His tardiness annoyed her, and she was about to leave when Prince Rainier arrived. He gave her a tour of the palace and they stopped to pose for pictures. By the time she left that afternoon she had the impression that this possible Prince Charming was indeed "very charming."

Be open to a "set-up":

When the film festival was over, Grace returned to her life in Hollywood, filming *The Swan*. That summer and fall she and Prince Rainier stayed in contact by exchanging letters. At year's end she went home to Philadelphia for the holidays, where she was reunited with Prince Rainier. He was ostensibly in town staying with friends of the Kellys, but everyone knew that this was no coincidence.

In an interview in 1957 Grace said that she nearly didn't go home for Christmas in 1955, having gotten a touch of cold feet about the matchmaking game waiting for her in Philadelphia. She feared that the expectations of those around them might make the reunion with Rainier awkward. "I can't

"I've been in love before, but never in love like this."

remember how it happened," she said, "I just went and bought a plane ticket anyway . . . [and] everything was perfect." Within a matter of hours of being reunited, they decided to marry. Just three months later, Grace was on her way to Monaco with the famous departing words, "I am going to fulfill my destiny."

"He's very sensitive and a very deep person. And besides, he's gorgeous."

The newly engaged couple, appeasing photographers.

Standing room only, amid the press in 1956.

"She'll make a lovely princess. What's past is past."

—Oleg Cassini

"He was the only guy in the world she could have married. Anyone else would have ended up being called Mr. Kelly. Not Rainier. He is a man's man . . ."

—Howell Conant, photographer and friend

Posing with Grace's parents, Margaret and Jack Kelly.

Beaming Grace and bemedalled Rainier at the Monte Carlo ball held at the Waldorf-Astoria Hotel just after their engagement in 1956.

A toast at the Monte Carlo ball.

"Grace believed in fairy tales and every young girl wants to grow up to meet Prince Charming. He found her and she couldn't believe her good luck . . ."

—**Arlene Dahl, actress and friend**

"When I was with him, I was happy wherever we were, and I was happy with whatever we were doing. It was a kind of happiness— well, it wouldn't have mattered where we were or what we were doing, but I'd have been happy being there and doing it."

Photographers snap away for a last shot of movie star Grace Kelly at the Oscars in 1956.

It's all about timing:

Perhaps there is no one perfect person for everyone. In Grace's life, it had much more to do with timing. In prior years she had been more focused on working to achieve her professional goals than on finding her life partner. Grace met Rainier at a time when both were able to recognize that each of them had the qualities they were looking for in the person with whom they could spend the rest of their lives.

"If I had met the prince two or three years earlier, perhaps I might not have married him—at least not so soon. But we came together at the right time. . . . It couldn't have been any different."

"This Prince is a wonderful person with a sense of humor. Grace has a good sense of humor, too. And they both love animals and music. She plays the piano. She is crazy about photography. And the Prince is a good photographer, too. And they are so in love. I have never seen Grace this way before."

—Rita Gam, Grace's friend

Be open to falling in love quickly:

Grace and Rainier had spent less than twenty-four hours in each other's company when they decided to marry.

Accept that love is risky business:

Grace on accepting Prince Rainier's marriage proposal: "It seemed right, and it felt right, and that was the way I wanted it. I knew that I was going to do it, and even if there was a chance I was making a mistake, I would find out later. Right then and there, nothing mattered to me except staying together."

Find common ground:

Asked what attracted her to Prince Rainier, Grace said, "Most things attractive in a person are things you cannot describe. He has a wonderful sense of humor, and we have the same religion. We seem to agree on most things."

With regal elegance, Grace was ever ready to become a princess.

CHAPTER EIGHT

Wedding of the Century:

Throwing a Memorable One

"A prince and a movie star. . . . It's pure fantasy"

—Aristotle Onassis

On $April$ 4, 1956, Grace—along with a group of about eighty, comprised of her bridal party, friends, and family—departed from New York harbor en route to Monaco. Every reporter on hand for the bon voyage wanted to know how she felt. "I feel very proud—not nervous," she said, "but I feel very anxious, as it is the most important event of my life." The trip across the Atlantic marked the last leg of Grace's old life. Her arrival in Monaco was followed by seven days of receptions and preparations for what the press and MGM publicists had titled the "Wedding of the Century." The events were covered by more than 1,500 reporters from all over the world.

A relatively intimate civil ceremony was held on the eve of the wedding in the palace throne room, with Grace wearing a pale pink two-piece dress. Soon she would bear the 142 new titles that came with being Prince Rainier's wife. Fireworks and a garden reception for the citizens of Monaco followed, all leading up to the official wedding day, April 19, 1956. The ceremony, held at Monaco's Catholic cathedral, was recorded for posterity by MGM cameramen. Permission to make the wedding an MGM production was a publicity coup arranged by the studio as a form of payback for losing Grace. She came away with a wardrobe in the deal. Costumes from *High Society* became part of her trousseau, and MGM designer Helen Rose supplied the $7,226 wedding gown that Grace wore on the big day. After the ceremony the

One of the first portraits of Prince Rainier and Grace.

couple cruised around Monaco in a Rolls Royce to greet the people as man and wife. The newlyweds finally escaped the media blitz by sailing away on their honeymoon aboard Rainier's yacht, *Deo Juvante II*, named for the Grimaldi motto, "With God's help."

"The day we left I felt as if I were sailing off into the unknown. I couldn't help wondering, 'What's going to happen to me? What will this new life be like?'"

Go by sea instead of by air:

Friends said the trip from New York to Monaco aboard the USS *Constitution* was like being away at camp for eight days, with programs of activities to follow and everyone in high spirits.

With her parents on the USS *Constitution*, en route to Monaco in 1956.

A promenade with her new Weimaraner, a wedding present.

Protect yourself:

The scene of her arrival in Monaco is a testament to Grace's ability to exhibit coolness under pressure. She was greeted by Rainier and a crowd of more than 20,000 people. Faced with her first taste of the adulation that would be directed at her as a princess, Grace handled it all with typical Kelly composure. She did have one prop to help her, however: she wore a wide-brimmed hat that partially obscured her face. The crowd hated it.

"I have heard the creator of Miss Kelly's hat has said she will never make another hat like it. It is the hope of everyone who saw that hat that she will keep her vow."

—Monsignor Joseph A. McCaffrey of Monaco

Grace arrives in Monaco—wearing the offending wide-brimmed hat that so upset the masses who wanted to get a good look at the future princess.

Mr. and Mrs. John Brendan Kelly request the honour of your presence at the marriage of their daughter

Grace Patricia

to

His Serene Highness the Prince of Monaco

Thursday, the nineteenth of April at half after ten o'clock in the Cathedral

Monaco

Dress Uniform, Frock or full formal Decorations

The favour of a reply is requested before April third to the Secretariat of the Palace and, upon arrival, this invitation should be presented because, in order to assure admittance cards.

Invitation to a wedding in Monaco.

Everyone has trouble with in-laws:

The Kellys and the Grimaldis met for the first time in the days prior to the wedding in Monaco. Unable to agree on basic levels of decorum, neither family approved of each other. The Kellys were unimpressed by titles and got the distinct impression that Prince Rainier's family felt superior to them.

The Kellys in turn unwittingly offended their intended in-laws with countless bits of what the Grimaldis perceived as impropriety, primarily based on dress and behavior. Peggy Kelly's choice to drink milk with her escargot, for instance, was sharply criticized by Rainier's mother, Princess Charlotte.

The couple at the reception following their civil ceremony, a day before the big official wedding day.

Choose your bridesmaids wisely:

Grace's entourage consisted of several women with whom she had been close for many years. She offered a spot in the lineup to her future sister-in-law, Princess Antoinette, unknowingly committing a breach of etiquette because it was simply out of the question for a member of the Grimaldi family to serve as a bridesmaid. Grace's offer was met with a cold response—proving it's best to stick with those you know and love for the bridal party.

The bridal party, April 19, 1956.

Grace becomes Her Serene Highness.

Find your dream dress:

Grace's bridal gown, crafted of yards of off-white Italian faille taffeta with rose point Brussels lace and embellished with small pearls, was designed by MGM's top designer, Helen Rose. Grace was consulted on all aspects of the gown, and it was everything she wanted it to be. David Evins designed a pair of classic rounded-toe, $2\frac{1}{2}$-inch high-heeled shoes for her to wear.

The bridal party witnesses the joining of Rainier and Grace in wedlock.

Decide if a big wedding suits you:

The elaborate nature of Grace's wedding turned horrific for both bride and groom, but they knew that they had no choice in their positions.

"It was so hectic and so quick and frantic. There was no time to sit and think about anything. Things just happened, and you reacted on the moment. It was kind of hard to describe the frenzy. . . . It was nightmarish, really."

"Grace kept saying: maybe we should run off to a small chapel somewhere in the mountains and finish getting married there. I wish we had, because there was no way either she or I could really enjoy what happened."

—Prince Rainier

"They hated the wedding. They never looked at any photographs for years. It was such a mob scene, and too many people, and they wanted to get married just together, with the family."

—Princess Caroline

Grace and Rainier exit the Cathedral of St. Nicholas after their wedding ceremony.

The newlyweds ride through the streets of Monaco in an open car.

Portrait of the resplendent bride and groom.

Choose a dream honeymoon:

Though generally on a far smaller scale than what Grace and Prince Rainier experienced, there are always many people around in the days preceding a wedding. A honeymoon should be very special, as it's the first chance for the couple to get away by themselves after the frantic weeks leading up to the wedding. The prince and princess escaped the wedding frenzy by taking a seven-week cruise around the Mediterranean.

A formal portrait of the couple dressed in their bridal best.

CHAPTER NINE

Hard Knocks:

Getting Through the Difficult Times

"The biggest change in my life wasn't the palace, it was the adjustment to marriage itself."

Perhaps the greatest sacrifice of Grace's life was giving up her life as Grace Kelly—including career, family, friends, country, and language—when she assumed her position as Princess of Monaco. And it all happened in such a short period that she had no time to prepare for these losses or for the new responsibilities she would assume—no time to become accustomed to royal protocol, a palace, the intense loneliness of having her loved ones far away, or for marriage in general.

". . . please let me know what you're doing and all the news and gossip you can think of. I love to hear what is happening where I am not."

—Grace in a letter to a friend in America shortly after her marriage

Find the right climate:

Some live by the saying "it's always fair weather;" others don't feel at the top of their game in certain climates. Grace and her northern roots preferred the cold. Monaco's semi-tropical weather never agreed with her.

"I get a dull feeling when it's hot and sunny. I feel tired. I don't want to do anything. I usually stay in the house when the sun is out. At night I take walks."

The frenzy that surrounded Prince Rainier and Grace from the time of their engagement made private moments between them few and far between.

"I like to walk in the rain. . . . When it's cloudy and damp, it's good."

Grace and Rainier with Prince Albert, Princess Caroline

Make your house a home:

Taking charge of a domestic staff consisting of scores of workers was no small feat. It also took a lot of adjusting for Grace to go from the apartments and homes she had known in America to the Medieval Italian palace of Monaco. The palace's trademark nineteenth-century clock tower was built around the time that it went from being a royal fortress to being a palace fit to house a family. It was not necessarily the perfect setting for a twentieth-century princess. Outmoded in many ways, a new wing equipped with modern conveniences for the family had to be built in 1968. The palace's rooms, estimated in the area of three hundred, reflected different cultures and eras,

but aristocratic French interior design was a common theme. The outdoor grounds included tropical plants, trees, and exotic gardens overlooking the Mediterranean, which Grace tended to as often as her duties permitted.

Giving gifts to the children of Monaco, Christmas 1966.

Play it cool:

More than anything, the scrutiny of the press tested Grace's composure; it made her truly uncomfortable. She was already famous as Grace Kelly, but the attention that came with being a Hollywood movie star was not as intense as the spotlight that shined on her as Princess Grace of Monaco. She had extraordinary poise and seemed perfectly at home amidst both the royalty of Hollywood and the crowned heads of Europe at different periods in her life, but it was difficult and more against her nature than she let on. She once said, "I'm basically a shy person. I don't like being with people I don't know. I had to get over that. It wasn't easy, but when you're thrown suddenly into a life like mine, you just do."

Maintaining privacy was something Grace valued intensely from the moment the press began to take an interest in her. Her pet peeves included having her thoughts misrepresented and being misquoted. She was candid but guarded in interviews, saying she always felt "a bit stiff" being herself rather than playing a role in front of the camera. Generally speaking Grace demonstrated the ultimate in calm, cool, and collected composure with the press throughout her life, an attitude that tended to engender respect in return.

"The freedom of the press works in such a way that there is not much freedom from it."

"Occasionally I think back to the days when I knew what it was to walk down a street and not have anybody know who I was."

Portrait of Her
Serene Highness.

"I certainly respect people who have a job to do, [but] some papers kind of feel that we're fictitious characters and that gives them the right to make up any kind of story they want, and one is helpless in defense of that."

Decide where your duties lie:

Among directors, actors, and every manner of studio technician who had enjoyed working with Grace, there was hope that she would be able to continue her career on a limited basis after she was married. Alas, it turned out to be only wishful thinking. As the previous year's Best Actress Oscar winner, Grace was to present the Best Actor Oscar in 1956. Handing Ernest Borgnine his award for *Marty* turned out to be her final act as a Hollywood star.

After they became engaged, Rainier told reporters, "Grace will give up her career. It is better that she does, and she thinks so, too. And it won't be necessary for her to work anymore." Grace said that she didn't mind leaving behind some aspects of Hollywood, such as the gossip and the early-morning wake up calls, but the void left by not performing increased in her as the years went by. Then in 1962 the perfect opportunity

Princess Alexandra, *The Swan.*

for her to return to acting was presented by her former mentor, Alfred Hitchcock, in the form of a script titled *Marnie*. As her children were no longer infants it seemed the right time. Prince Rainier was amenable to the idea, agreeing that they could go to America together with the children that summer. Grace intended to donate her salary to a children's charity.

Good cause or not, in Monaco acting was not highly regarded and Grace had to politely decline Hitchcock's invitation to return to the screen. The handwriting had been on the wall since 1956, when it was proposed that *High Society* have its premiere in Monaco and a palace source told the press, "It just wouldn't be right to have the princess being shown in the arms of one man tonight and another tomorrow, even on the screen."

"The idea was not pleasing to public opinion. It judged that [acting again] did not conform with my capacity as a princess. . . . It is in Monaco that my first duties lie."

"Thank you dear Hitch for being so understanding and helpful. I hate disappointing you. . . . I also hate the fact that there are probably many other "cattle" who could play the part equally as well. Despite that I hope to remain one of your "sacred cows."

—Grace Kelly to Alfred Hitchcock, making reference to the director's famous remark comparing actors to cattle

"I would love to act, but it is not possible. I have duties as a princess and a mother."

The prince and princess of little girls' daydreams.

"I loved working at my craft. I didn't like having to have the public appearance of being a movie star, although even in Hollywood my private life was pretty much my own. When I married, my private life became public and I really had no privacy at all, and that was an adjustment to make."

Keep a hand
in what you love:

If something stands in the way, find a way around it. In the years after the *Marnie* disappointment, Grace would have a chance to quench her thirst for acting in other ways, including participating as herself in the film *Poppies Are Also Flowers* and narrating the documentary *The Children of Theatre Street* in 1977. In the late '70s she also began a series of poetry readings in Europe and America.

"She just lit up before the camera. You could tell it was a wonderful and moving moment for her. The extraordinary thing is she looks better today than she ever did. There is an excitement in her face now, a marvelous maturity."

—Terence Young, director of *Poppies Are Also Flowers,* in 1966

"She looked after everybody from the makeup person to the electricians. . . . She just enjoyed being with a film crew again and knowing that everybody there adored her and respected her."

—Robert Dornhelm, director of *The Children of Theatre Street*

Holding a poppy in a publicity shot for *Poppies Are Also Flowers*, 1966.

Embrace your roles in life:

Some could balance marriage and children with a career. Grace was unable to as an actress, but in marrying Rainier she wasn't just following a dream to become a wife and mother; she also assumed the career of Princess of Monaco. It was not her first choice as a career, but she proved that there can be satisfaction in making the most of a second choice—in Grace's case taking an active role in the revitalization of Monaco.

"It's a small world all its own. There's always a crisis, or a problem. Of course it gets tiresome. Yes, I sometimes feel hemmed in, very hemmed in. But I have a full, active life. I don't ever waste time wishing for what I can't have. I think looking back with regrets is macabre and destructive. I love acting. I'll always miss acting. I was a very ambitious actress, but I was also very ambitious to be a wife and mother. Some women worked it out to have both. It didn't work out that way for me."

"I respect what she did with her career and also the choice she made for the man she loved."

—Princess Stephanie

Remember no one leads a fairytale existence:

Grace said that the first years of her marriage to Prince Rainier were the happiest, though he had a moody temperament, perceptible from the start, that often put her off-balance. The '70s was a particularly difficult period for them. They kept up a beautiful façade of having a perfect marriage, but they grew apart, having fewer shared interests. He was consumed with affairs of state; she was heavily involved in charity work, her children's lives, and in the arts community. Keeping up appearances was important to Grace and, she felt, part of her responsibility to the people of Monaco. Appearances can indeed be deceiving. It's worth remembering that the fabulous-looking young couple across the street has their difficulties too.

Prince Rainier and Grace at Roc Agel, 1979.

"I've had happy moments in my life, but I don't think happiness—being happy—is a perpetual state that anyone can be in. Life isn't that way."

Don't distance yourself:

In the mid-'70s, when Grace took a home with her children in Paris, where the girls went to school, she and Rainier spent less time together, and there were rumored infidelities on both sides. Close friends said that the '80s seemed to be a turning point in their relationship, when they began to show that their love was still strong and focus on each other again. They say "absence makes the heart grow fonder," but there seems to be more truth in the statement that nothing hurts a relationship like distance. Sadly, the sparks only reignited in the last years of Grace's life. After losing her, Rainier expressed the normal regrets any spouse would have—mainly he wished they had had more time together.

"My life and the lives of so many have never been the same since the day this wonderful woman entered my world. I adore her more today than ever before. She is my Princess, and I salute her."

—Prince Rainier, toast to Grace on their twenty-fifth wedding anniversary

Prince Rainier escorts Grace to a performance of *Amadeus* on Broadway, June 1981.

CHAPTER TEN

Dial M for Motherhood:

Advice on Parenting

"Woman's natural role is to be a pillar of the family."

Princess Grace with Prince Rainier

Nine months and four days after her wedding day,
Grace and Prince Rainier presented the citizens of Monaco with their
first child, Princess Caroline, born January 23, 1957. It was not the boy
that was hoped for—the people would have to wait a little over a year for the
arrival of Prince Albert. A third child, Stephanie, came in 1965. Grace always
wanted to have children; she adored them and would have had more if she
had been able to. She suffered through multiple heartbreaking miscarriages
in the 1960s. Grace never got to meet her grandchildren, all of whom were
born after her death.

Prince Rainier holds Caroline, Grace their son and heir, Albert, in 1958.

"If children are to grow up stable and strong, and make a reasonable world, it has to begin with a loving, responsible mother and father, a close family, physically and emotionally. Where else is a child to learn respect for authority, consideration for other people—a regard for decency? It all begins with a close family who loves one another."

The proud parents with firstborn daughter Caroline.

Reading to Princess Stephanie.

"I guess I was a dreamy, imaginative child. I never gave my mother any trouble. I was usually over in a corner, talking to myself, playing my own games. My children are the same way. They usually play near me, and I'm not really listening to them, but I know they are there. It's background music in my ears."

". . . things are more liberal, more open, freer today. One good side of it that I see is that people are able to discuss more openly things that used to be hidden with great pains in the past. Growing up has never been easy, has it?"

"It would be very sad if children had no memories before those of school. What they need most is the love and attention of their mother."

"I hope we have love and respect for one another, and I think we are friendly enough that we can discuss almost anything, but your mother's not going to be your best pal."

—Grace, speaking of Caroline

Prince Rainier and Grace pose with their children on the cover of the magazine that brought them together by arranging their first meeting, *Paris Match*.

Realize you can't always protect them:

Intrusion of the press was always the bane of Grace's existence. Her children began having their exploits documented from the time of their births, particularly Grace's headstrong and beautiful daughters. Seeing Stephanie climb into the trunk of a car to avoid reporters on her way to gymnastics class was very difficult to bear. Grace would say she understood that she and her husband were public figures, but felt strongly that her children ought to be protected. There was really nothing that she could do about it, being who she was and her children being who they were.

Grace with Prince Albert, age six, and Princess Caroline, seven.

A family portrait on Rainier and Grace's tenth wedding anniversary, 1966.

Don't expect them to follow in your footsteps:

Grace saw firsthand the enormous amount of pressure put on her brother by their father, who looked to John Jr. to succeed where he had been unable to compete by taking first place at the Diamond Sculls in Henley, England. Grace never tried to steer her children into acting as a profession—and they had no interest in trying to fill her shoes, at least not as an actress.

Mother and daughters Stephanie, age four, and Caroline, twelve.

"I tried out for a school play once. I made everybody laugh. I forgot my lines, and I ended up pulling the curtains. Acting? Absolutely never. Then I'd be compared to my mother."

—Princess Caroline

Let them live and learn:

Princess Caroline's first husband, Philippe Junot, was seventeen years her senior and had a reputation as a playboy. Against her parents' objections she married him in 1978, and then divorced him two years later. Stefano Casiraghi, an Italian sportsman whom she married in 1983, was the father of her three children. Their marriage was ended by his death in a speedboat racing accident in 1990. On her third try at marriage, Caroline married a prince in a union that has lasted for more than ten years. Today she is settled as the wife of Ernst August V, Prince of Hanover, making her Princess of Hanover.

Prince Albert was destined to assume Prince Rainier's sovereignty and became Prince of Monaco upon his father's death in 2005. However, because he has not yet produced a legitimate heir, Princess Caroline's children are the hereditary heirs to Monaco.

Stephanie, whom Grace called her "wild child," has been at times a designer, model, and singer. Her romances have been making headlines from about the time she was thirteen and continue today. She had two children fathered by her bodyguard, Daniel Ducruet, in the early 1990s, and she

A family portrait in 1976.

Grace and Caroline in 1959.

married him in 1995. They were divorced the following year. She had been in the car during the accident that took her mother's life in 1982. While it is true that in the preceding days Grace and then seventeen-year-old Stephanie had been arguing about Stephanie's desire to live with her boyfriend at the time, whispers that Stephanie was behind the wheel during the accident are false.

"I suppose Caroline must obey her heart at that age. I know I always did."

—Grace on Caroline's marriage to Philippe Junot

"You try to convince yourself you don't care what people say, but it hurts. You know, my mom died and everyone said I was responsible. You're already in grief of losing a loved one, and suddenly everyone points at you. And it's like they're saying, Why is she still around?"

—Princess Stephanie

Let them know
where you came from:

Living in Monaco, Grace felt it was important for her children to get a taste of the American values that she had grown up with, besides getting their European education. She wanted them to know and understand where both of their parents came from. French was their first language, but Grace spoke to them in English. As they grew older the children were enrolled in private schools in England and France.

"I try to incorporate [American] traits into my children's upbringing. For example, the hospitality for which Americans are so well known. People here are not hospitable in that way. You can know a Frenchman for twenty years and never be invited to his home. He will entertain you very handsomely at a restaurant, but you won't see the inside of his house."

"The emphasis on sports may be carried too far in American schools, but there must be a happy medium. Here, there are not as many team sports, and I think that is unfortunate. It is so important for a child to learn to play on a team, to learn teamwork. Learning to get along with the other fellow—that's a basic in life today."

Giving Back:

Becoming a Perfect Do-Gooder

"Grace is a woman who must keep on topping herself.
It's the way she is. . . . one fact I am sure:
Grace will never be happy standing still."

—William Holden

By 1956 Monaco had earned a reputation, in the words of Somerset Maugham, as "a sunny place for shady people." Grace was the best thing that could have happened to Monaco at a time when its very future as an independent land was at stake. A treaty with France stipulated that should a reigning Grimaldi fail to produce an heir, the principality would be annexed to France and its people would be subject to French taxes. After Princess Grace of Monaco arrived, tourism dollars and property values increased dramatically and the number of daily visitors skyrocketed. Most importantly, together with Prince Rainier, she presented the principality with its necessary heir.

Beyond those first accomplishments, in her twenty-six years as princess, Grace transformed Monaco's international reputation as a glorified pleasure principality into that of a cultural center for tourists, a glittering "Jewel of the Riviera" where fairytales come true.

Princess at a costume ball.

"Royalty above all represents a continuity that is important in all lives . . . and I think that a lot of the troubles today stem from the fact that young people don't know who they are and need that feeling of tradition."

Grace in 1955.

"She showed from the first a natural aptitude for being a princess, a quality of belonging that I've found to be rare in people suddenly risen to such a position."

—Elsa Maxwell, famous society hostess

Be generous with your time:

Grace took her role as Princess of Monaco with as much earnestness and passion as she led her acting career. She used her position to do as many good works as she could possibly handle. Grace became president of the Monaco Red Cross and as such took the time to review every single case. She was devoted in her work with the Sainte-Devote girls' shelter. She worked with committees to preserve historic sites of Monaco. She assisted at the retirement home and hosted Christmas parties for the orphans' home. As a member of the World Association of the Friends of Children, she aided and supported children across the globe. She worked tirelessly for the La Leche League, an organization that encourages natural childbirth and breastfeeding. Grace also opened a boutique in Monaco that employed a staff of about sixty people, many of whom were invalids without other opportunity to display and sell their wares. On a more global level, Grace was honored by the United Nations for her work to end world hunger. As the glamorous focal point at countless gala fundraisers, she helped raise millions for her favorite charities. Finally, she left a lasting legacy in the Princess Grace Foundation, an association that continues to sponsor emerging talents in the performing arts.

JOURS DE FRANCE

LA PRINCESSE GRACE

N° 698 - 1,50 F
30 MARS 1968

240

"Monaco is so small, you see, the Prince and I are involved in every-thing. There is nothing that goes on that we're not a part of. The activity is constant; there's never an end."

"Idle hands are the devil's playmate."

Looking radiant at a costume ball in the 60s.

—One of Grace's favorite sayings

"I was touched that [the La Leche League] asked me to be their speaker, and I went because it is all a part of my feeling that the best contribution I can make right now is whatever I can do to make it a better world for the children."

"Grace was very honorable. She would not promise something and not do it. She was very precise, very professional, never late, always on time. . . . Once Grace said she would do something, she would do it. She wouldn't get involved in a charity unless she was going to do something about it."

—Jay Kantor, Grace's friend and former agent

Take time for yourself:

Grace loved to get away to reenergize at the family "House of Happiness," a vacation home at Roc Agel.

"Roc Agel is where we close the door to the world."

Have a hobby:

From the time a friend introduced her to the art of pressed flowers, Grace was hooked. She created countless collages, and a collection of them was even put on display at a gallery in Paris.

Connect with people:

In large kingdoms members of the royal family are distant figures; within the principality of Monaco, comprised of less than five hundred acres, Grace took every opportunity to create a family feeling.

"I believe in the individual and I think the individual is important and here we're able to deal with individuals."

Portrait of a down-to-earth princess circa 1975.

CHAPTER TWELVE

Saying Farewell:

And Leaving
Fond Remembrances

*"I'd like to be remembered as
a decent human being . . . and a caring one."*

On a September morning in 1982 Grace prepared to take the wheel of her Rover 3500 to drive down to Monaco with Princess Stephanie from the family's country home in the heights of Roc Agel. Grace was weary. Teenaged Stephanie had plans to move in with her boyfriend at the time, Paul Belmondo, the son of the actor Jean-Paul Belmondo, and there had been many mother-daughter quarrels. Physically Grace had also not been feeling well for some time, suffering from severe headaches and experiencing intensely unpleasant effects of menopause. The winding road ahead of them was as treacherous as one could imagine, like the scene between Grace and Cary Grant winding down the mountain in *To Catch a Thief.* At the worst curve, the Rover swerved and went over an embankment. When the car crashed to the ground, Grace was knocked unconscious and then fell into a coma. She had suffered brain damage, and it was determined that it was due to a stroke or an aneurysm that precipitated the accident. The following day, September 14, 1982, Grace was gone. Her funeral service was held in the cathedral where she had been married, and she was laid to rest in the Grimaldi family vault.

Diamonds, furs, and a studied balance of shadow and light—as glamorous as can be.

Age gracefully:

Grace died at fifty-two, never reaching old age, but her words show that she would have faced the strain the years have on the body inside and out with her usual grace.

"It is a question of facing the inevitable and not getting upset about it. One doesn't feel older until you start getting aches and pains and have to curtail or adjust your activities. That hasn't happened to me—yet. I'm lucky and am just looking forward to what comes next."

"I avoid looking back. I prefer good memories to regrets."

"I didn't find her vain at all. She was proud of every wrinkle she had."

—Robert Dornhelm, Grace's friend

An aging Grace, with her magnificent bone structure intact, retaining her beauty.

Leave behind
warm memories:

Grace left a lasting impression on almost everyone she met. Some were dumbstruck by her beauty, some she had helped in her many charitable activities, still others were enthralled by the short but impressive film legacy that she left behind, but it was her friends who knew her best.

"Grace is so natural and unaffected you can't help liking her. . . . She lets people warm up to her gradually. . . . She's just herself and anyone who meets her falls in love with her."

—Wally Westmore, makeup artist and friend

"She is beautiful and she is regal. . . . She is reserved, but one has the feeling that one can get to know her— she has the marvelous art of being able to put herself over that so many American woman seem to have."

—Prince Tasilo, relative of Prince Rainier

"I'd say she is one of the finest young actresses on the American stage or screen today, but more important, she is the type of girl who will always be a credit to her family and her background."

—John Ford, director of *Mogambo*

"[Princess Grace] touched the lives of countless people, not only in the United States, but in nations across the world, with her wonderful talent and charm and her generosity of spirit."

—Nancy Reagan

"I adored her. She was thoroughly and constantly considerate of other people first. As far as I was concerned, she was a princess long before she married [Prince Rainier]."

—Celeste Holm, *High Society* co-star

In her *Dial M for Murder* period.

With her great friend James Stewart, who delivered the eulogy at her memorial service in Hollywood.

"You know, I just loved Grace Kelly—not because she was a princess, not because she was an actress, not because she was my friend, but because she was just about the nicest lady I ever met. Grace brought into my life, as she brought into yours, a soft, warm light every time I saw her, and every time I saw her was a holiday of its own."

—James Stewart

"I would like to be remembered as someone who accomplished useful deeds and who was a kind and loving person. I would like to leave the memory of a human being with a correct attitude and who did her best to help others."

—Grace Kelly, 1982

Grace beams at her sister's wedding reception in 1955.

Bibliography

Associated Press, March 30, 1956.

Associated Press, January 8, 1956.

Balaban Quine, Judith. *The Bridesmaids*. New York: Weidenfeld & Nicolson, 1989.

Boston Sunday Globe, July 2, 1989.

Diehl, Kay and Digby. *Remembering Grace*. New York: Time Inc., 2007.

Dherbierm Yann-Brice and Pierre-Henri Verlhac, *Grace Kelly: A Life in Pictures*. London: Pavilion Books, 2007.

Grace Kelly, 1982. ABC News Productions, Inc., 2007.

Grace Kelly: American Princess. Hearst Entertainment, Inc., 1995.

Grace Kelly: Hollywood Princess. A&E Television Networks, 1999.

Haugland, H. Kristina. *Grace Kelly*. New Haven and London: Philadelphia Museum of Art/Yale University Press, 2006.

International News Service, April 12, 1956.

International News Service, April 18, 1956.

Lacey, Robert. *Grace*. New York: G. P. Putnam's Sons, 1994.

Leigh, Wendy. *True Grace*. New York: Thomas Dunne Books, 2007.

Mitterand, Frédéric. *The Grace Kelly Years*. Monaco: Skira Editore/Grimaldo Forum Monaco, 2007.

New York Daily News, January 11, 1956.

Philadelphia Bulletin, January 14, 1954.

Philadelphia Bulletin, November 7, 1954.

Philadelphia Bulletin, March 20, 1955.

Philadelphia Bulletin, April 16, 1956.

Philadelphia Bulletin, July 23, 1971.

People, August 30, 1976.

People, September 21, 1992.

Prince's Palace in Monaco. A&E Television Networks, 1998.

Taraborelli, J. Randy. *Once Upon a Time*. New York: Warner Books, 2003.

Time, January 31, 1955.

United Press International, January 4, 1956.

Photo Credits

Page 1: © Allan Grant//Time Life Pictures/Getty Images

Page 2: © Hulton Archive/Getty Images

Page 16: © Archive Photos/Hulton Archive/Getty Images

Page 29 (bottom): © Lisa Larsen/Time Life Pictures/Getty Images

Page 93: © Howell Conant/Bob Adelman Books

Page 109: © Phillippe Halsman/Magnum Photos

Page 140: © Howell Conant/Bob Adelman Books

Page 172: © Ralph Morse/Time Life Pictures/Getty Images

Page 188: © Rolls Press/Popperfoto/Getty Images

Page 191: © Howell Conant/Bob Adelman Books

Page 197: © Howell Conant/Bob Adelman Books

Page 201: © Reg Birkett/Hulton Archive/Getty Images

Page 203: © Howell Conant/Bob Adelman Books

Page 209: © AFP/Getty Images

Page 212: © Howell Conant/Bob Adelman Books

Page 218: © AFP/Getty Images

Page 220: © SSPL/Getty Images

Page 223: © Time & Life Pictures/Getty Images

Page 225: © Popperfoto/Getty Images

Page 231: © AFP/Getty Images

© Temple University Libraries, Urban Archives, Philadelphia, PA: back cover, pages 6, 18, 19, 20, 21, 22, 25, 26, 28, 29 (top), 33, 34, 35, 36, 37, 38, 39, 40, 44, 45, 46, 47, 51, 53, 59, 104, 105, 106, 126, 130, 132, 133, 134, 135, 138, 142, 143, 144, 145, 147, 148, 155 (bottom), 159, 168, 171, 176, 178, 179, 180 (bottom), 181, 183, 195, 222, 250, 253.

Courtesy The Lou Valentino Collection: pages 13, 98, 101, 102, 103, 124, 151, 158, 165, 205, 224, 226, 229, 237, 240, 241. © MGM: pages 8, 10, 12, 42, 49, 61, 62, 63, 66, 72, 73, 74, 75, 88, 89, 90, 94, 95, 96, 110, 112, 113, 114, 115, 116, 118, 119, 121, 122, 129, 141, 150, 234, 238, 244. © Paramount: pages 100, 163.

Courtesy Photofest: pages 156, 167, 169, 170, 175, 182, 192, 196, 198, 202, 208, 216. © Paramount: cover.

Courtesy author's collection: pages 15, 30, 127, 128, 139, 161, 180 (top), 187, 193, 194, 199, 200, 204, 206, 211, 214, 219, 227, 228, 243, 248. © MGM: pages 5, 64, 71, 92, 117, 125, 146, 152, 155 (top), 247. © United Artists: 54, 55, 56, 58, 87. © Warner Bros.: 68, 69, 70, 131, 137, 157, 164, 184. © Paramount: 77, 78, 80, 81, 82, 83, 84, 85, 86, 91, 99, 107, 108, 149, 232, 252.

Any omissions or errors that may have been made in photo credits are unintentional. If notified, the publisher would be pleased to amend in future editions.

Acknowledgments

Getting to thank my fabulous family, friends, and coworkers is one of my favorite parts of the book-writing process. This book was a departure for me made possible with the help and support of many. First of all, my mother and father are the best; they are quick to call whatever I do great and it makes me venture to prove them right.

At Running Press: I am grateful to Jon Anderson for acquiring this book and to Chris Navratil for your faith in it as Publisher. Greg Jones, you are the best boss ever, period. Jennifer Kasius, my editor, you inspire me to be a better writer and a better editor. Corinda Cook, I marvel at your design. Dan Clipner, thank you for overseeing this on the Production end.

Among my other favorite people: Trisha, my BFF sister. Manny, Jess, Michael, the perfect little family. Frankie, you started by reminding me that I had dropped my Grace Kelly idea and ended up "all over this book." Thanks for the inspiration. Jordana—so loyal and so fun, you are the best friend a girl could have. Melissa, you inspire by having more than a touch of Grace. To my grandmothers, Tristan, Jenny, Geri, Cara, Betsy, Kimmy, Lou, Angie, Erick, Steve, Bridget, Joe, Darina, Maria, everyone at Running Press (Seta, Kristen, Whitney, et al.)—thank you for being my ever-supportive and *beautiful* friends and family.

To the staffs of the Academy of Motion Picture Arts and Sciences, the New York Public Library, the Free Library of Philadelphia, and Temple University's Urban Archives.

And to my greatest inspiration of all, Grace Kelly. Thank you.

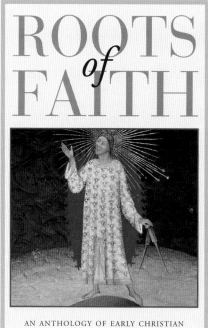

ROOTS *of* FAITH

AN ANTHOLOGY OF EARLY CHRISTIAN
SPIRITUALITY to *contemplate* and TREASURE

EDITED BY

ROBERT VAN DE WEYER

WILLIAM B. EERDMANS PUBLISHING COMPANY
GRAND RAPIDS, MICHIGAN

Compilation © 1997 Hunt & Thorpe
New Alresford, Hampshire SO24 9JH, UK
Text © 1997 Robert Van de Weyer
Picture research by Lynda Marshall

This edition published 1997
through special arrangement with Hunt & Thorpe by
Wm. B. Eerdmans Publishing Co.
255 Jefferson Ave. S.E., Grand Rapids, Michigan 49503

Printed in Hong Kong

ISBN 0-8028-3751-4

Designed and produced by
THE BRIDGEWATER BOOK COMPANY LTD

Picture Acknowledgments
BRIDGEMAN ART LIBRARY
page 9 Museo dell'Opera Del Duomo, Prato;
page 11 British Museum, London;
page 31 National Gallery, London;
page 41 Musée Conde, Chantilly;
page 51 City of Bristol Museum and Art Gallery;
page 69 De Morgan Foundation, London;
page 79 Prado, Madrid;
page 98 De Morgan Foundation, London.

E. T. ARCHIVE
pages 2, 7, 59, 89, 109, 119

FINE ART PHOTOGRAPHIC LIBRARY
page 21

CONTENTS

INTRODUCTION

CHRISTIANITY is now an old religion, encrusted by tradition. And the writings that comprise the New Testament are so familiar to us, and so burdened by the interpretations that are placed upon them, that it is difficult to recapture the youth and vigor of the faith they describe. But there is a body of writing, virtually unknown to modern readers, that can still convey to us the freshness of early Christianity. Collectively, the writers are usually known as Apostolic or Early Fathers, and some of them knew the apostles personally. Indeed, when the New Testament was formed late in the second century, some of their works were considered for inclusion on the grounds that they had apostolic authority.

Fresco from the Sta Maria del Carmine chapel, Florence, depicting St. Peter distributing the goods of Ananias after his breach of the rules of the community (Tommaso Masaccio, 1401–29).

The New Testament itself bears witness to the spread
of Christianity across the Roman world in the decades
following the death of Christ. And we gather from the Book
of Acts that Peter and Paul were both martyred. We also hear
of divisions within the Church, most notably at Corinth,
and there are strong hints of heresy,
especially in the epistles of John. All these
features are magnified in the Early Fathers.
Evangelistic zeal is undimmed, and the gospel
penetrates every corner of the Roman
Empire. And from the time of Emperor Nero,
when he blamed Christians for the great fire
of Rome, this new religion became a
convenient scapegoat for all manner of ills:
it even became a crime to bear the name

"Christian." Religious fervor within the churches made internal divisions, especially over questions of leadership and authority, virtually inevitable.

This collection includes extracts from almost all the Christian writings that have survived from the last years of the first century to the end of the second. Along with the New Testament, they comprise the roots of the Christian faith. And their form mirrors that of the New Testament. Some are public letters to churches, like those of Paul; some are letters to individuals, like those addressed to Temolty; some are spiritual reflections, like the writings of John; there is a piece of historical description, similar to those in the Book of Acts; and there is an apocalypse, as in the Book of Revelation. Only one form is original, the "apology" written as a defence against persecution, and as a justification of Christianity to non-believers.

If the New Testament remains the most exciting collection of Christian writings, the works of the Early Fathers are not far behind. Like the New Testament, they express the freshness of the new faith, and they also contain insights which are as true and relevant today as they were then. The Early Fathers are not read nearly as widely as they deserve; this book is an attempt to put that right.

ROBERT VAN DE WEYER

CLEMENT
OF ROME

CLEMENT was the leader of the Church in Rome in the last decade of the first century. He had probably been a slave in a Christian household in which the husband was martyred by Nero. After his conversion Clement was set free. His letter to the Church in Corinth was prompted by news reaching Rome that, as in Paul's time, the Corinthian Christians were divided, with rival groups following different leaders. Clement was not a great theologian, nor a man of passion, but saw Christianity primarily as a moral movement, whose central feature should be the pure and holy lives of its believers. In writing to Corinth he was not asserting the dominance of Rome, but saw himself as a loving brother offering advice. The second letter ascribed to Clement may be by a later hand, but continues with the same tone and attitude.

The Ancient of Days *by*
William Blake (1757–1827).

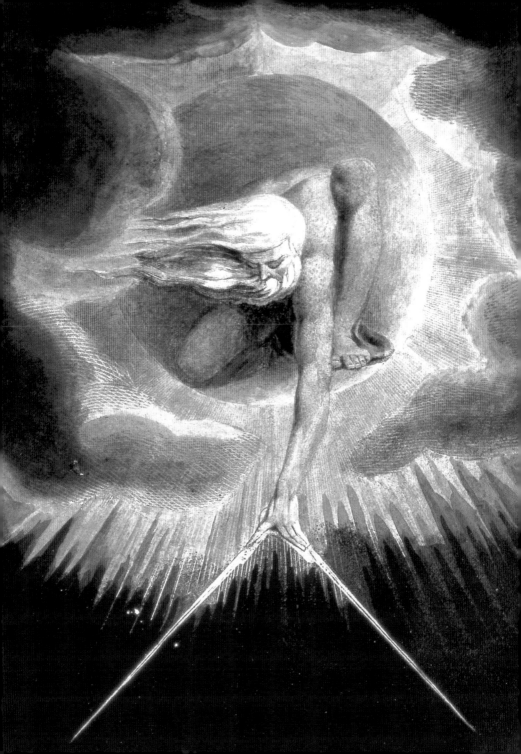

I

IAPOLOGIZE for the delay in dealing with the issues disputed amongst you, and especially the alien ideas which a few rash and self-willed people amongst you have been spreading. Once you were renowned for the peace and goodwill that reigned within your community; but now that reputation is sullied by your bitter conflicts. Who amongst your guests has not testified to your virtues and your steadfast faith? Who has not admired your seriousness of purpose and your quiet piety? Who has not reported your generous hospitality? Who has not blessed your profound wisdom? You acted always without regard for personal status, but did only what was righteous in the eyes of God. You taught your children the simple and gentle ways of Christ. Your womenfolk were blameless and pure, showing warm affection for their husbands. And your menfolk were humble, free of all arrogance, and always more ready to give than to receive.

1ST EPISTLE OF CLEMENT TO THE CORINTHIANS: CHAPTER 1

II

THE Holy Spirit was poured out in abundance on you all, giving you a rich and profound sense of peace, and also an insatiable desire to do good. You were full of holy plans, and with childlike trust you opened your arms to God, praying to him for all your needs. Day and night you strove to add to the number of God's elect, urging those around you to submit to his mercy and compassion. You were utterly sincere, with no guile, and bore no malice towards one another. As if by instinct you rejected any ideas foreign to the truth, and conflict was unthinkable. You mourned over the misery and the sin of your neighbors, as if that misery and sin belonged to you. And you offered help to your neighbors without any thought of the cost to you. You were true citizens of God's kingdom, and his laws were written on your hearts.

1ST EPISTLE OF CLEMENT TO THE CORINTHIANS: CHAPTER 2

III   LET us remember two men who have recently fought long and hard in the battle between good and evil. Peter lost faith under trial and deserted the path of righteousness; but his faith returned, and he testified to numerous people of the glorious mercy of God. Paul persecuted the faithful, but then found his way to the path of God. Seven times he was chained, exiled, and stoned, yet he remained true to his vocation as a herald of the gospel across the world, and his noble faith became famous from the East to the West. He talked to rulers and to peasants with equal respect and passion, desiring only to open their hearts to God's truth. Peter and Paul are both wonderful examples to us of how wickedness can be overcome, and righteousness reign: and both are now taken up to the Holy Place, which is their just reward.

1ST EPISTLE OF CLEMENT TO THE CORINTHIANS: CHAPTER 5

VIII Do not be irritated or angry when someone corrects you, turning you from evil to goodness. Sometimes we do wrong without knowing it because we are double-minded: we can deceive ourselves into thinking that evil is good. Equally do not be irritated or angry when you see sinful people enjoying great wealth and luxury. They are winning the contest for this world's prize, but we are running in the race for a far greater prize. The righteous person does not win his reward quickly, but must wait for it. This is because we have to train hard and long in order to win the race. After all, the crown of eternal life cannot be won easily with little effort; the person who wins it must have every spiritual muscle at the peak of fitness. It does not matter if you are weak in the affairs of commerce and trade, and so live in poverty. What matters is that you are strong in the affairs of the soul.

2ND EPISTLE OF CLEMENT TO THE CORINTHIANS
CHAPTERS 19 & 20

IGNATIUS
OF ANTIOCH

IGNATIUS was bishop of the Syrian city of Antioch – where, according to the Book of Acts, the believers were first called Christians – in the first decade of the second century. He was tried and condemned to death in his own city, but taken to Rome to be thrown to the wild beasts in the amphitheater. During the long journey under guard through Asia Minor, Christians from throughout the province came to meet him. He in turn wrote letters of encouragement for them to take to their churches. He also wrote to the Church in Rome to warn of his impending arrival. His letters reveal an anxious man lacking social grace, and yet filled with spiritual joy. His central concern is the unity of the Church, and he stressed the role of the bishop as a focus of unity and discipline. He has often been quoted over the centuries by the advocates of strict authority in the Church.

St. Cecilia, the patron saint of music, who was martyred by the Romans in the 2nd–3rd century (John Melhuish Strudwick, 1849–1937).

I

ISEND my greetings to the Church in Ephesus, which is blessed with the fullness of God, and which was destined from the beginning of time to share in his eternal glory. It is God himself who has told me of your faith and love. You are true imitators of God, living according to the natural laws of righteousness that he has written in your hearts. I write to you not as someone who is superior to you, because, although I am now a slave to God, I am not yet perfect in Jesus Christ. I am learning to be a true disciple, and I look upon you as fellow learners. You can teach me much about faith and endurance. Equally my love for you prompts me to speak honestly to you about how to live in harmony with God. As a pastor, my task is to convey the will of Jesus Christ, which is the will of the Father.

EPISTLE OF IGNATIUS TO THE EPHESIANS: CHAPTERS 1 & 3

I I THUS it is right that you should live in harmony with the will of the pastor, as indeed you do. The leaders amongst you, who are truly worthy of God, are attuned to me as their pastor like strings on a harp. So, by the loving harmony between us, Jesus Christ is being sung. Let each of you join fully in this choir, that you may receive the note you should sing from God himself, and so proclaim Jesus Christ with the most wonderful spiritual music. Let the Father hear you through your good works, and so recognize you as brothers and sisters of his Son. The prayer of one person on his own has great power, but the prayer of a whole church in unity with its pastor has power beyond telling. So let no one separate himself from the assembly, imagining that he can do better alone; such a person is guilty of the sin of pride. It is as humble members of a great spiritual choir that we learn truly to love and praise God.

EPISTLE OF IGNATIUS TO THE EPHESIANS: CHAPTERS 4 & 5

III THERE are some who appear to be true and worthy preachers, but whose hearts are full of guile and whose minds are full of falsehood. In fact, I have learned that people of this kind have actually stayed with you and preached their evil doctrine. These men are like wild beasts who attack you from behind when you are off your guard; and once you are bitten by them, it is hard to be cured. Stop your eyes to them, and chase them from your midst. And if you have been bitten, turn to Jesus Christ, who is the one physician able to heal both soul and body, because he is both God and man, born of God and Mary. To change the image, these false preachers are like hurricanes that can blow you off course. Your faith is like a windlass by which you are held on course; and your destination is the eternal love of God, which brings perfect joy. So ensure that your faith is strong and will not break, by constant prayer and good works.

EPISTLE OF IGNATIUS TO THE EPHESIANS: CHAPTERS 7 & 9

I V IT is better to be silent and be real, than to talk and be unreal. Teaching is good, if the teacher practices what he advises. The best teaching is not by words but by example. He who truly possesses the words of Jesus Christ in his heart hears those words constantly within the silence of his heart; and his every action expresses Christ's love. Nothing is hidden from Christ, for he can read our innermost thoughts. So let us do all things as if he were dwelling within us, that we may be his temples, and our actions become like hymns of praise. Beware false teachers, whose mouths are filled with eloquent words but who do not know the words of Jesus in their hearts. Only accept the teaching of those whose lives demonstrate the truth of what they are saying. Better to hear no verbal teaching at all than to risk hearing words of corruption. Each of you who knows Jesus can hear his words within your heart and can teach others by your action.

EPISTLE OF IGNATIUS TO THE EPHESIANS: CHAPTERS 15 & 16

V

I AM tempted sometimes to boast about my own knowledge of God and to take pride in my position. But I know to give way to such temptations would prove that in truth I had nothing to boast about. It is better for me to be timid and diffident in what I say, and to ignore those whose admiring words puff me up. Those who speak to me in that way are a scourge to me. I desire to suffer for Christ's sake, but I do not know whether I am worthy to suffer. The devil is constantly at my heels, even though other people imagine me free from temptation. So I ask you to pardon me if anything I say seems motivated by pride. Indeed, I believe it is when my words become complex and I try to speak with cleverness, that pride distorts what I say. True teaching is simple, and the heart that knows the truth has no need for complex ideas. So listen to me only when I speak with simplicity.

EPISTLE OF IGNATIUS TO THE TRALLIENS: CHAPTERS 4 & 5

V I You have never envied anyone, but only taught people the way of Christ. I desire only that I may stay firmly on that way. Please pray for me, that I may have both spiritual and physical strength to perform my duties; that I may not only speak the truth, but become the truth; that I may not only be called a Christian, but also live like a Christian. Yet I do not want people to look to me as an example, for at best I can only be a pale reflection of Christ Jesus; let people look away from the reflection and turn to the reality. Christianity is not a matter of persuading people of particular ideas, but of inviting them to share in the greatness of Christ. So pray that I may never fall into the trap of impressing people with clever speech, but instead I may learn to speak with humility, desiring only to impress people with Christ himself.

EPISTLE OF IGNATIUS TO THE ROMANS: CHAPTER 3

VII   I AM traveling from Syria to Rome, by land and sea, by night and day, guarded by ten soldiers whom I call leopards. The more kindly I speak to these leopards, the more cruelly they treat me; and by their cruelty I am becoming a more devoted disciple of Christ. I long for the wild beasts that are prepared for me, and I pray that when I arrive I shall be taken quickly to them. Once with the beasts I shall entice them to devour me quickly; if they seem unwilling, I shall force them to it. Grant me this favor: pray that nothing will stand in the way of my suffering for Christ. I shall happily have my skin cut to shreds by the beast's teeth, my limbs torn from by body, my bones mangled in their jaws, my whole body crushed under their feet, that I may come to know Jesus. The wealth of this world counts for nothing; to be king of every nation on earth is worth no more than a few specks of dust. All that I desire is to die for the sake of the one who died for our sake.

EPISTLE OF IGNATIUS TO THE ROMANS: CHAPTERS 5 & 6

VIII The Prince of this world wants to tear your souls to pieces, and turn your minds away from God towards him. Let none of you help him through deceit and hypocrisy. Do not speak warmly of Jesus Christ, and yet still lust after the things of this world. Do not let envy divide you. While in the midst of life, learn to desire death, because in that way all craving for material things will be crucified. Instead of wanting fine wine to indulge your palate, pray for the water of life to slake your spiritual thirst. Instead of wanting rich food to fill your stomach, pray for the bread of life to satisfy your spiritual hunger. Do not look for status or glory on this earth, but seek only the good opinion of God himself. Desire God alone, that he may desire you, and so guide you into his eternal kingdom. Listen to me not because I am your chosen pastor, but because as someone who is shortly to die I have no reason to deceive you: as death approaches, the truth is all that matters.

EPISTLE OF IGNATIUS TO THE ROMANS: CHAPTERS 7 & 8

III

SHEPHERD
OF HERMAS

IN the second century, many churches had this
extraordinary work as part of their scriptures,
believing it to have apostolic authorship. Like the Book
of Revelation, which was included in the final canon, it
probably dates from the very end of the first century or
the beginning of the second; and it shares the same
visionary and apocalyptic form. But, unlike Revelation,
its real purpose is practical and ethical. It consists of a
series of dreams, whose meaning is explained by a
mysterious shepherd. In these dreams, the author, who
calls himself Hermas, learns both the commandments of
God and the nature of the Church. The central theme is
repentance: that once a person has turned to Christ and
received baptism, he must reject all sin and become pure
in all his thoughts and actions. The visions, although at
times simple and even crude, are extremely vivid; and
the Shepherd's teaching shows the high moral idealism
of the early Church.

The baptism of Jesus in the River
Jordan by John the Baptist (Piero
della Francesca, c. 1419–92).

I   WHILE I was sitting on my bed at home, praying to the Lord, a wonderfully handsome man appeared. He was dressed as a shepherd, with a white coat made of goatskin, a bag over his shoulders, and a staff in his hands. He sat down beside me on the bed, and said: "I am your companion, the closest friend you have, sent by the Lord." I thought at first he was deceiving me; I wondered if he were a thief or even a murderer, so I shook with fear. "Do not be afraid," the man said, "I have been with you since you were born." "But I have never seen you before," I said. "You have not seen me," he replied, "because you have not been ready to see me. Every person that is born into the world has a companion sent by the Lord." His voice seemed strangely familiar; and I realized it was just like my own, but clearer and stronger. And his features seemed familiar, also; and I realized his face was just like my own, but more radiant and joyful. "I am you," the man said, "as God wants you to become. When you become like me, I will leave you."

SHEPHERD OF HERMAS: PART 4, CHAPTER 4

I I   LOOKED intently at the man dressed as a shepherd, who was sitting on my bed. "Why has the Lord chosen to reveal you to me now?" I asked. "It is because your ears are now open to hear deep truths, and your eyes are now open to see deep mysteries. You feel weak, but I will give you strength. You feel foolish, but I will give you wisdom. My purpose is to instruct you in all the matters that you already know in your heart. I will give you commandments, and I will unfold parables. Although you are illiterate, you will be able to write down what you hear and see; the Lord himself will move your hand across the page. You must keep all the commandments, repenting your past sin, and remaining from now onwards pure and blameless. Then you shall receive the reward that the Lord has promised. But if you do not keep the commandments, you shall receive the opposite of a reward." Then the shepherd began to dictate the commandments, and I wrote them down.

SHEPHERD OF HERMAS: PART 4, CHAPTER 5

III   FIRSTLY, believe that God is one. Divine power is all
around you. It is God who makes the corn grow
and the trees come into leaf each spring. It is God who
makes the fish swim and the deer leap. It is God who
causes people to laugh and cry, to sing and dance. God
manifests his power in an infinite number of different
ways; he reveals himself in an infinite number of different
forms. So sometimes people think there are many gods,
one god for each sign of divine power. But there is only
one God. He created all things, and is himself uncreated.
He contains all things, and is himself uncontained. He
sustains all things, and is himself uncontained. He
sustains all things, and himself needs no sustenance. He
will perfect all things, and is himself perfect. Believe in
him and fear him; and let fear bring self-control, so you
shall cast off the garments of wickedness and dress
yourself in righteousness.

SHEPHERD OF HERMAS: PART 5, CHAPTER 1

I V SECONDLY, be as simple and innocent as a little child. Do not try even to understand how evil minds and hearts work, because if you understand you will be tempted to imitate. Do not fill your head with complex theories about God and the heavens, because no human ideas can penetrate the divine mystery; God has revealed enough of himself for each of us to love him with all our hearts. Speak evil of no one, and do not listen to those who speak evil of others. If you listen to those speaking evil, you share in their sin, and you find yourself believing what they say. Do not respect the rank or status of others, but treat all as equals. Give generously and without hesitation when you see others in need, because God wants his gifts to you to be turned into gifts from you to others. Do not keep an account of what you have given, and leave it to others to give an account to God of what they have received from you. When you yourself need the kindness of others, receive their gifts with gratitude; but, just as you are not superior to those to whom you give help, do not feel inferior to those from whom you receive help.

SHEPHERD OF HERMAS: PART 5, CHAPTER 2

V

THIRDLY, love truth. Let all the words that come from your mouth be truthful. In this way your own heart will become truthful, and the spirit of the Lord will be able to dwell there. Those who tell lies are not only defrauding those to whom they speak, but they are defrauding themselves and God. Each person is offered by God the spirit of truth; and those who lie are throwing that gift back to him. There are many merchants and other men of business who think that lies and fraud will bring them prosperity; and they seek to compensate for those lies by being honest in matters unconnected with business. Those who wish the Spirit of God to dwell in their hearts must be honest at all times in all circumstances; and God will cause the honest man of business to prosper according to his needs. Yet there are some who are gripped by an evil conscience, imagining themselves to be liars and cheats, when in fact they are honest with themselves, with others, and with God. It is for each person to look very carefully at himself, to assess whether he is honest or false. And if he is honest, he should ask God to give him a peaceful and tranquil heart.

SHEPHERD OF HERMAS: PART 5, CHAPTER 3

V I   FOURTHLY, keep your minds free of impure thoughts. Many imagine that only deeds can be sinful and that thoughts escape judgment. But it is evil thinking that causes evil action, so sin must be rooted out of the mind if our deeds are to be righteous. A man must not desire another man's wife, and a woman must not desire another woman's husband. If one partner commits adultery, and later truly repents, then the other partner must remain faithful. But if a partner commits adultery, and does not repent, then the other partner would become a participant in the sin by preserving the marriage. When a husband or wife commits adultery, and does not repent, the other partner should leave the marriage and live alone. The way to avoid adulterous or any other kind of evil thought is to open your heart to the Holy Spirit and allow the Spirit to fill your heart with divine joy. The pleasures of the flesh will seem trivial, and temptation will melt away. A man who has once known the joy of God will never want to jeopardize it by entertaining evil thoughts, even for a second.

SHEPHERD OF HERMAS: PART 5, CHAPTER 4

VII FIFTHLY, be courageous and yet prudent, and you will always do what is right. If you are courageous, the Holy Spirit who dwells within you will be pure, not obscured by the evil spirit of fear. Courage enables us to seize the opportunities for righteousness that God provides, while fear causes us to draw back. God will always reward acts of courage, so we need not be frightened of any danger. Fear oppresses the soul and chokes all good intentions; the person filled with fear knows what is right but fails to act.

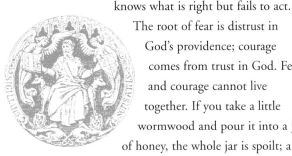

The root of fear is distrust in God's providence; courage comes from trust in God. Fear and courage cannot live together. If you take a little wormwood and pour it into a jar of honey, the whole jar is spoilt; a very great quantity of honey can be ruined by very little wormwood, taking away its sweetness. In the same way a small degree of fear can undermine courage. Yet courage must be tempered with prudence, so that courage does not turn into impetuosity. Consider carefully each opportunity as it arises, praying for God's guidance on how to act; and when in prudence you have decided what is right, act decisively.

SHEPHERD OF HERMAS: PART 5, CHAPTER 5

VIII

SIXTHLY, control your temper so that it is directed only to what is good and right. Ill temper can destroy even the best of actions. It enters the hearts of people, making them feel bitter about even the most trivial matters; and it destroys friendship, by turning small mishaps into causes of deep resentment. Ill temper starts with foolishness: a person responds excessively to some incident. From foolishness comes bitterness, from bitterness comes wrath, from wrath comes rage, from rage comes fury; and fury leads to the most terrible sins, including even murder. The man who is prone to ill temper finds himself dragged in all directions, from one cruel act to another. Yet the same quality of passion, which can lead to ill temper, can also engender the most wonderful acts of righteousness. The heart with a burning passion for righteousness can defy and destroy every evil in this world. The person of righteous passion is always gentle and kind with those who are weak and vulnerable, because his anger is directed towards those who oppress them. And far from being the enemy of peace, the passion of righteousness ultimately brings harmony in relationships between people, and tranquility within the soul.

SHEPHERD OF HERMAS: PART 5, CHAPTER 6

BARNABAS

THE writer of this epistle was known by many in the early Church to be the apostle Barnabas. But this could not be proved to the satisfaction of the compilers of the New Testament canon and so it was excluded. The author was probably a Christian living in Alexandria. Nonetheless, the epistle dates from apostolic times and may even have been written as early as A.D. 70. The author was probably a Jew, who criticizes his fellow Jews for failing to see that the coming of Jesus Christ was prophesied in the Old Testament. He also offers wise and delightful instructions for those newly converted to the Christian faith.

The tortures of the damned in Hell as depicted in the fifteenth-century Tres Riches Heures du Duc de Berry.

I   GREETINGS, sons and daughters of the almighty Father; may his love and peace be with you. I rejoice at your generous and warm-hearted spirit, which God has instilled within you; you have truly been born anew in his love. When I look upon you, and see the glorious blessings that God pours out on those who are saved, I congratulate myself on my own salvation; the sight of you is the promise of what I will become. Since I was with you I feel the Lord has traveled with me on my journeys, guiding my feet in the way of righteousness. And as I have come to know the Lord a little better, I have grown to love you even more dearly, cherishing you above my own life. And out of that love I want to share with you some of the insights that I have received – hence this short letter. It is a privilege for me to be able to minister to such noble spirits as yours.

EPISTLE OF BARNABAS: CHAPTER 1

11   THERE are three central aspects of Christianity. The first is the hope of eternal life, which is the beginning and end of our faith. The second is righteousness, which is the beginning and end of judgment. The third is joy, which is the beginning and end of love. Through the resurrection of Jesus Christ, we have had a glimpse of what is promised for all who are saved, because he is the first fruits of the harvest of salvation. Through the example of Jesus Christ in his life and work, we understand righteousness, and by following his example we can be sure of favorable judgment. Through the joy that Jesus mediates, which originates in his perfect heart of love, we want to share that joy and so grow in his love. We live in evil days, and the prince of evil is in power in the world. Thus we need to hold fast to our hope, our righteousness, and our joy, granted to us by God in Christ, that we may resist all evil, and finally rise to eternal life.

EPISTLE OF BARNABAS: CHAPTERS 1 & 2

III IN these last days our life and our faith will profit us nothing, unless, as sons and daughters of God, we can ensure that the Evil One has no entry into our hearts or our fellowship. Let us avoid all vanity, because it is by appealing to our sense of pride that the Evil One can more easily seduce us. Do not try to live alone, away from your fellow disciples, as if you were already righteous; instead, stay close to each other, because together your spiritual strength is multiplied. Strive to keep the commandments of Christ with punctilious precision, never trying to make excuses or exceptions, because only in this way can you stay on the straight and narrow path that leads to eternal life. No matter what your position or status is on earth, you will be judged by the same standards as everyone else, because God is no respecter of worldly status. Be constantly vigilant; do not rest content with yourself as you are, but, night and day, strive to be more like Christ. The person who slumbers in his sin will die in sin; the person awake to righteousness will live in righteousness.

EPISTLE OF BARNABAS: CHAPTER 4

I V

WE have been created anew in Christ Jesus; our hearts of stone have become hearts of flesh. In truth, Jesus himself lives within our hearts, so our bodies become temples of his Spirit. And he also lives amongst us, binding us together in love. In days of old the Hebrew people were promised a land of milk and honey. We have now received the true and eternal milk and honey. A child is first nourished with milk, and then with honey. In the same way, Christ nourishes us with spiritual milk when we first come to faith, feeding us the aspects of the truth that we can understand. Then he begins to feed us the spiritual honey of divine joy, pouring his love into our souls until we are overflowing with praise and thanksgiving. Yet like a loving parent, God not only feeds us, but also guides and disciplines us, showing his anger when we do wrong so that our souls are filled with remorse. God rules over the birds and the wild animals, the flowers and the trees, showing his love for them by determining how they should grow and live. His love for us is far greater, so his commands are far stricter.

EPISTLE OF BARNABAS: CHAPTER 6

V

As far as possible and as simply as possible, let me try to summarize what is necessary for salvation. I do not want to write in parables, but in plain words. There are two ways: the way of light and the way of darkness. And there is a great difference between these two ways. Along the way of light stand the angels of God, radiating his brightness. Along the way of darkness stand the angels of Satan, casting their shadows over the path. The way of light goes from eternity to eternity; the way of darkness from iniquity to iniquity. To follow the way of light a person must study carefully the commandments of God, and follow them precisely. Anyone who does this shall enjoy the eternal light that shines from God's throne, because for all eternity he shall sit in God's presence, basking in his light and praising his glory. But anyone who follows the way of darkness shall perish.

EPISTLE OF BARNABAS: CHAPTERS 17,18 & 21

V I

THE way of light is a journey to a destination chosen by God. And to make that journey you must follow God's directions, which are these: you shall love and fear God as your creator, and you shall glorify him as the one who redeemed you from death. You shall be simple in heart and rich in spirit. You shall not mix with those who work in the way of death, and you shall hate all that is not pleasing to God. You shall reject men who are hypocritical, and you shall always be honest and sincere. You shall not try to exalt yourself or take any glory to yourself for what you achieve, but be humble, boasting only in God's power. You shall not make malicious plans against your neighbor. In your conversation you shall never say things contrary to God's Word, even if this provokes hostility. You shall be indifferent to men's status, opposing sin wherever you find it and whoever commits it. You shall be meek and quiet, listening carefully to everything men say, in order to discern God's wisdom in their words.

EPISTLE OF BARNABAS: CHAPTER 19

VII   IF you wish to follow the way of light, you shall love your neighbor more than your own life. You shall cherish your sons and daughters, teaching them to love and fear God. You shall not abort the unborn child in order to avoid the duties of parenthood, nor murder infants, but rejoice in every child as a gift from God. You shall not be greedy and envy your neighbor's possessions. You shall not seek out powerful and wealthy men as your friends, but prefer instead the friendship of the humble and the righteous. Whatever suffering and hardships befall you in the course of life, you shall accept these as sent by God, knowing that nothing happens without God. You shall not be two-faced or unduly talkative. You shall obey those in authority over you, so long as what they command is in accordance with God's commands. And you shall be gentle and merciful in giving commands to those under your authority, since servant and master are equal in God's sight, with the same hope of salvation.

EPISTLE OF BARNABAS: CHAPTER 19

VIII IF you wish to reach the destination God has
appointed for you, then you shall regard nothing in
your possession as belonging to you, but everything as
belonging to God. Thus you shall be willing to share all
things with your neighbor, knowing that your reward
shall be spiritual wealth that can never rust or decay. You
shall not push forward your own opinions,
but seek in all matters to discern the will
of God. You shall love and cherish as
the apple of your eye all who speak
to you about God, guiding you
along the way of light. Day and
night you shall remember that life
on earth is a preparation for the life
to come; and thus you shall live and
act day and night in the anticipation
of God's judgment. When
opportunities arise to help others, you
shall not grumble, but rejoice in the
prospect of pleasing God. You shall avoid all quarrels over
earthly matters, but work together with others in earning
God's approval. You shall never worship God with an evil
conscience, but always confess any sins and make amends
before worshipping God, so you can come to him with a
pure heart. This is the way of light.

EPISTLE OF BARNABAS: CHAPTER 19

POLYCARP OF SMYRNA

POLYCARP was Bishop of Smyrna for the first fifty years of the second century. He came from a patrician family and was respected throughout the city by nonbelievers as well as by his flock. As a young man he had been a disciple of John the Divine, the author of the Book of Revelation. His Epistle to the Philippians was written in about the year 125. It was prompted by news that one of the leaders of the Philippian congregation had been embezzling church funds. His words reveal a receptive rather than a creative mind, in which the preservation of good order and the teaching of sound doctrine are primary concerns.

The Virgin Mary adoring the newborn Christ (Jacopo del Sellaio, 1441–93).

I   I REJOICE greatly with you in our Lord Jesus Christ, that you have followed the pattern of true love, and have helped one another in the ways of righteousness as opportunity has arisen. Once you were prisoners of sin; now you are jewels in the crown of life. I rejoice, too, that you have remained firmly rooted in the faith for so many years. Your initial spiritual fervor when the seed was first sown was famous throughout the world. Now that seed has grown into a strong, robust tree bearing succulent spiritual fruit. And this fruit attracts newcomers to taste it, so they too come to enjoy the rich grace of our Lord.

I write to you now not because I am worthy to offer you guidance, but because you have invited me to write. I cannot emulate the wisdom of the apostle Paul, who taught you so accurately the truth about Christ, both in speech when he was among you, and in letters when he was absent. It is better that you study his words, which will build up your faith, than pay attention to what I can write.

EPISTLE OF POLYCARP TO THE PHILIPPIANS: CHAPTERS 1 & 3

I I REMEMBER that we bring nothing into this world, and can take nothing out. So we should put no trust in material riches, but only in spiritual treasures; and metal armor cannot save us from evil, but only the armor of righteousness. Those of you who are wives should love your husbands not with lust but with gentle concern for their spiritual wellbeing; and you should educate your children in the fear of God. Those of you who are widows have a special opportunity to give the same chaste love that you once directed to your husbands to the whole church. Let the husbands among you protect your wives from all evil, be firm in directing your sons and daughters in the way of righteousness, and be examples of spiritual strength to all. And all of you should avoid slander, false witness, love of money, and every kind of evil. For each of you is an altar on which every action, every thought, and every feeling is offered as a sacrifice to God.

EPISTLE OF POLYCARP TO THE PHILIPPIANS: CHAPTER 4

I I I

LET your pastors be blameless in all matters – temperate, compassionate, scrupulously honest, and the servant of everyone. What you do for God in the world you shall receive back from him a hundredfold in the life to come. Your duty as a pastor is to bring back those whose minds and hearts have wandered from the truth, to care for the weak and vulnerable, to ensure that the poor among you have ample food and clothing, and in all things to treat everyone with equal love and respect. Do not be hasty in judgment, or quick to show anger, but be patient and calm, trusting always in the judgment and the power of God. Day by day, pray to God to forgive you for the ways in which you failed in your duties, asking him for greater strength in the future. And as soon as you become aware of an error or sin you have committed, do not try to hide it, but confess it openly, asking the forgiveness of those in your care.

EPISTLE OF POLYCARP TO THE PHILIPPIANS: CHAPTERS 5 & 6

I V

CHRIST is our hope, and in that hope we find courage to persevere through all trials, temptations, and hardships. Let us imitate the endurance of Christ, who suffered and died for our sake. Remember Ignatius, Zosimus, and Rufus, as well as Paul himself, who suffered and died for their faith in Christ. They did not run the course of life in vain, but in death they received the crown of glory. When you feel weak in the faith, draw closer together for mutual support, that together you may be strong. When your mind becomes distracted by worldly concerns, concentrate your attention on the needs of others and work even harder to satisfy those needs. Above all, do not allow your faith to be perverted by false teaching. There are always people who are prepared to pervert the words of Christ for their own purposes, and to deny the final judgment in order to persuade themselves and others that they can sin without fear of punishment. Do not even listen to such people, but turn your back on them.

EPISTLE OF POLYCARP TO THE PHILIPPIANS: CHAPTERS 7, 8 & 9

V

SOME believers claim that the sufferings of our Lord Jesus Christ were not real, but a kind of fantasy. They argue that a man who is divine could not truly suffer; and that they themselves, if they share in his divinity, will also escape suffering. What they are saying is that Christ was not truly clothed in flesh, but that his body was a kind of corpse, a lifeless thing that gave the appearance of a body. And this leads them to imagine that they can enjoy the resurrection to eternal life without sharing in the crucifixion; that their sins do not need to be nailed on to the cross with Christ. In fact, they regard themselves as sinless. Beloved brethren, be on your guard against these falsehoods. You may be tempted to believe these lies, but they will lead you to hell. Jesus Christ was born of a human mother, with a body of flesh like ours; and in flesh he rose to life. After his resurrection he even asked the disciples to touch him, to prove that he was no ghost, but truly flesh.

EPISTLE OF POLYCARP TO THE PHILIPPIANS: CHAPTER 14

V I

THOSE who deny the humanity of Christ Jesus also deny all human standards of morality. They are indifferent to love, they have no care for the widow and the orphan, they feel no compassion for the sick and the distressed, they see no reason to give food to the hungry and water to the thirsty, they have no concern for the prisoner. And they abstain from the eucharist, because they deny that the eucharist signifies the flesh of our Saviour Christ Jesus; in their eyes he had no flesh, so the eucharist is meaningless to them. They even deny the power and purpose of prayer, because even this they regard as an indulgence of the flesh; for them life in Christ is purely spiritual, so he cannot give material help in answer to prayer. These people are not in themselves wicked, for they hold their beliefs with great sincerity. But the beliefs lead to great evil and must be firmly rejected. Such people must be forbidden to speak in public and in private, and must be excluded from the fellowship.

EPISTLE OF POLYCARP TO THE PHILIPPIANS: CHAPTER 15

THE MARTYRDOM
OF POLYCARP

IN the year 155, Polycarp fell victim to local persecution. The account of his martyrdom is apparently written by an eyewitness and is the oldest account of such an event. It compares Polycarp's death with that of Christ. Like his master, Polycarp did not wish to defy the authorities and made little effort to avoid arrest. At his trial he was sharp and direct in his answers, without any histrionics; and in death he was serene and dignified. His behavior came to be regarded as a model for Christians facing persecution.

An eighteenth-century painting showing St. Laurence being roasted on a gridiron (Hipolito de Rioja).

I

POLYCARP, when he first heard about the persecutions, was not disturbed or worried, and wanted to remain in the city. But the other Christians persuaded him to leave quietly, and he went to live on a farm a short distance away, where he enjoyed the company of fellow believers. There he prayed night and day for the churches throughout the world, and especially for Christians threatened with persecution. And while he was praying he fell into a trance which lasted three days, in which he saw the pillow under his head burning, with flames rising from it. When he awoke from the trance, he declared: "I must be burned alive." Yet far from giving himself up to the authorities, he continued to try to escape them. Soldiers looking for him went from farm to farm. And when Polycarp heard that they were near the farm where he was staying, he quietly left at the dead of night and moved to another farm. He knew that God wanted him to die a martyr; but in obedience to God he tried to escape martyrdom.

THE MARTYRDOM OF POLYCARP: CHAPTER 5

11   WHEN the soldiers arrived at the first farm where
Polycarp had stayed, they arrested some young
slaves there and began to torture them in order to extract
information. One of the slaves broke silence under
torture and told the soldiers where Polycarp had gone.
Thus it proved impossible for Polycarp to escape. The
soldiers, whose captain was called Herod, went to the
house where Polycarp was staying. They were carrying
their full arms as if they were advancing against an enemy
army. They arrived at the house one Friday evening at
suppertime, and found Polycarp praying in an upper
room. Even at this late stage he could have climbed out
of the window and fled, but he remained quietly in the
room, saying: "Let the will of God be done." Then when
he heard the soldiers coming into the house, he went
downstairs to talk to them. He was an old man, and even
the soldiers felt ashamed at carrying their full arms to
arrest such a person. Polycarp ordered that the soldiers be
given food and drink, and asked if he could have an hour
to pray without interruption. The soldiers agreed, and
while they ate their fill, Polycarp praised God. The
soldiers' shame deepened as they heard the fervent
prayers of this vulnerable disciple of Christ.

THE MARTYRDOM OF POLYCARP: CHAPTERS 6 & 7

I I I A s Polycarp was brought by the soldiers into the city, a voice came from heaven: "Be strong, Polycarp, and play the man." And as he was led through the city, and people saw that he had been arrested, there was a great uproar. Polycarp was brought before the proconsul, who asked if he was indeed Polycarp. The old man affirmed his identity, and immediately the proconsul tried to persuade him to deny his faith. "Respect your age," the proconsul said, urging him to spare his old bones the torment of a violent death. Polycarp  said nothing, and the proconsul grew irate, shouting at him: "Swear by the genius of Caesar that you refute your atheistic religion." Polycarp still remained silent. The proconsul now lowered his voice and said in mock gentleness: "You need only say 'Away with the atheists,' and your life will be saved." Polycarp now waved his hand towards the crowd of pagans that stood around and said: "Away with the atheists." This spurred the proconsul to even greater anger. "Take the oath and revile Christ," he yelled. Polycarp replied: "For eighty-six years I have been his servant, and he has done me no wrong. How can I blaspheme my King who saved me?"

THE MARTYRDOM OF POLYCARP; CHAPTER 9

I V

T HE proconsul persisted in his attempts to persuade Polycarp to renounce his faith, urging him to swear allegiance to the emperor. "If you imagine I will swear allegiance to the emperor," Polycarp said, "then you are ignorant of who I am. Listen plainly: I am a Christian. And if you wish to learn the doctrines of Christianity, let us arrange a day, and I will teach you." The proconsul replied, "Teach the people, and win them for your doctrines." "I will teach anyone who asks," Polycarp said, "and I will be especially pleased to teach you because you are a man who has been taught to honor the truth, and to respect princes and governors appointed by God." But the proconsul grew impatient, and said, "I have wild beasts that I will set on you, if you do not repent." Polycarp answered "Call for your wild beasts, because it is impossible to repent from better to worse, but only from evil to righteousness." "If you despise wild beasts," the proconsul said, "I will cause your body to be consumed by fire." "You threaten me with fire that burns for a few minutes or hours and is then quenched." Polycarp replied, "but you do not know the everlasting fire that awaits the wicked."

THE MARTYRDOM OF POLYCARP: CHAPTERS 10 & 11

V

POLYCARP could see no object in remaining with the proconsul. "Why are you waiting?" he asked. "Do what you will, and quickly." Polycarp's heart now filled with courage and with joy, and his face became radiant with divine grace. Not a trace of fear or anxiety could be seen in his expression. The proconsul was astounded at Polycarp's appearance. He sent his herald to the middle of the arena to announce three times: "Polycarp has confessed that he is a Christian." When the herald had finished his announcement, the heathen and the Jews assembled there cried out in uncontrollable anger: "This is the father of the Christians, the destroyer of our gods, who turns people away from offering sacrifices." And they urged Philip, the keeper of the wild animals, to let loose a lion on Polycarp. But Philip could not legally do this because the official Sports had ended. So instead they shouted out that Polycarp should be burned alive. This was how Polycarp's vision, in which he saw his pillow burning under his head, was fulfilled.

THE MARTYRDOM OF POLYCARP: CHAPTER 12

V I

MATTERS now moved with great speed, quicker than it takes to relate them. The crowd gathered wood and bundles of twigs from the workshop nearby, and assembled them in a great heap; in the middle they put a large stake. When the fire was ready, Polycarp took off his outer garments and tried to take off his shoes. But other Christians nearby, eager to touch his flesh for the last time, rushed forward to take the shoes off his feet for him. Despite their anger, the crowd treated him with honor out of respect for his age. So instead of dragging him to the fire, they led him gently, and put his back against the stake. They were about to tie and nail him to the stake so that he could not escape the flames. But he pleaded with them not to do so. "Leave me like this," he said, "because he who gives me power to endure the fire will give me strength to remain here unmoved. So I do not need the security of your rope and nails."

THE MARTYRDOM OF POLYCARP: CHAPTER 13

V I I   **P**OLYCARP finished his final prayer with a loud cry of "Amen." Then the men in charge of the fire lit it, and instantly great flames arose around the venerable old man. Those of us who were privileged to see this fire witnessed a great marvel; and we thank God that he has preserved us, so we can report what we saw. The flames formed the shape of a room. It was as if a great wind was blowing from Polycarp, so that the flames, like the sails of a ship, were blown outwards. Thus the fire formed a wall around Polycarp, but did not burn his flesh. He was like bread being baked in the oven, or like silver and gold being refined in a furnace: he was not harmed, but was being made ready to be offered to God. And from the fire a strong sweet fragrance arose that the whole crowd could smell: it was like the aroma of incense and other costly spices.

THE MARTYRDOM OF POLYCARP: CHAPTER 15

VIII   **F**INALLY, Polycarp's murderers, seeing that his body had not been consumed by the fire, decided that he should be stabbed to death. So, as the flames died down, one of their number took a sharp sword and pierced Polycarp in the breast. From the wound a dove emerged and flew upwards towards heaven. And then so much blood gushed forth that the fire was completely quenched. The crowd was astounded at what it witnessed. Some were moved to even greater heights of anger and hatred against the saint and his faith, but many began to wonder if there was indeed truth in the doctrines that Polycarp had proclaimed. The body of Polycarp was still upright, standing against the stake; and although it was now lifeless, it was clear to everyone that the flesh was entirely unharmed. His friends in the crowd almost believed that the saint would walk from the fire and return to our midst. But as the dove disappeared into the clouds, we knew that Polycarp's soul had been carried to God.

THE MARTYRDOM OF POLYCARP: CHAPTER 16

DIDACHE

THE manuscript of the Didache, or the Teaching of the Apostles, was unearthed in the Library of the Patriarch in Constantinople as recently as 1875. It describes, in unique detail, the life and liturgy of the early Church. Scholars have hotly debated its date. Some put it as early as A.D. 100, since it describes the Church in a formative stage, when the rule of bishops was not yet established and itinerant prophets still played a major role. Other scholars put it half a century or more later, suggesting that it relates to a remote church away from the main centers. At all events, it gives us the first account of the celebration of the Eucharist after the description in Paul's Epistle to the Corinthians; and some of the imagery is very powerful.

The principle of Christian charity is shown in Jesus' parable of the widow's mite, depicted here in a sixth-century Italian mosaic.

I

THERE are two Ways, the Way of Life and the Way of Death, and there is a great difference between the two ways. The Way of Life consists in loving God, who made you, and loving your neighbor as yourself; and whatever you would not like done to you, you do not do to others. The Way of Life consists also in blessing those who curse you; praying for your enemies; fasting on behalf of those who persecute you; loving those who hate you; giving your possessions to those who need them; refusing to accept any goods or money that you do not need; reflecting constantly on your sins and seeking to make amends; and blessing the vulnerable and the innocent. The Way of Death consists in committing murder, adultery, and sodomy; in stealing, indulging in magic, aborting fetuses and killing babies; in telling lies and accumulating wealth you do not need; in speaking evil of others; in being double-minded and double-tongued; in hypocrisy of all kinds; in making evil plans against others; and in hating others.

DIDACHE: CHAPTERS 1 & 2

I I

MY child, avoid all evil people, because you can be far more easily influenced by their words and actions than you imagine. Do not be proud, because pride leads to jealousy and conflict. Do not be lustful, because lust leads to fornication and adultery. Do not take notice of omens and astrological predictions, because this leads to idolatry, in which the universe is worshipped instead of its Creator. Do not tell lies, because lies lead to every other kind of dishonesty, such as stealing and scheming. Do not love money, because this, too, leads to theft. Do not grumble, because this leads to blasphemy. Do not be stubborn, because this leads to division. Do not think evil of others, because this leads them to think evil of you. Do not practice guile, because this leads you to deceive yourself. Do not seek the company of the powerful, because they will use you for their own purposes, but prefer the company of the humble. And when events occur which upset you, regard them as gifts of God, because nothing happens without God.

DIDACHE; CHAPTER 3

I I I   MY child, remember in your heart and in your prayers those who teach the Word of God to you, and honor them; because wherever people speak truly about the Lord, he is present amongst them. Each day, seek out the company of saintly men and women, that you can find peace in their words. Do not get caught up in any plans for division and schism within the Church, but try to reconcile those who oppose one another. When you see evil, be courageous in speaking against it, regardless of the status of the evildoer. Do not stretch out your hands to receive gifts, yet do not close your hands when it comes to giving. Whatever you have gained by the work of your hands, over and above your own needs, you should give away as a ransom for your sins. You should never hesitate when you give, nor grumble when you do so, but share everything willingly with your brother. Remember that nothing really belongs to you, but everything belongs to God.

DIDACHE: CHAPTER 4

I V

IF a teacher arrives in your midst, and teaches you these truths, receive him gladly. But if the soul of the teacher is perverted, and he is saying things opposed to these truths, then close your ears to him. The test is whether the words of the teacher lead to an increase in righteousness and knowledge of the Lord; if so, welcome such a teacher as the Lord. When a traveling preacher or prophet comes to you, receive him graciously as the Lord. But do not let him stay more than one day, or two at the most; if he asks to stay three days, he is a false prophet. And while he is with you, give him food and drink; but if he asks for money, he is a false prophet. The surest way to know whether a teacher or a prophet is genuine is by his behavior. If he does not do as he preaches, then he is false. But if his actions reflect perfectly his doctrine, then he is true.

DIDACHE: CHAPTER 11

V

LET everyone who comes to you in the name of the Lord be welcomed warmly. Yet be on your guard, because even those who profess the faith most devoutly may be liars and thieves. Those Christians who travel from place to place should be given food and shelter for two days, or three at the most, and then be asked to continue on their journey. When a Christian asks to settle amongst you, then he should be made to work for his bread. If he has a craft, then he should practice that; if not, give him work according to his ability. No one should live in idleness amongst you just because he is a Christian. A person who refuses to work, or says he will work but proves lazy, is making a mockery of Christ; beware of such people.

DIDACHE: CHAPTER 12

V I EVERY true prophet and teacher who settles amongst you is worthy of his food; so is every workman. The true prophets in particular should be treated with great respect, for they are the mouthpieces of God. As a sign of respect, take the first batch of wine from the wine-press and the first loaves from the harvest, and the first ox and sheep to be slaughtered, and give them to the prophets amongst you. If there are no prophets with you, give them to the poor. Similarly, when you open a new jar of oil, pour out the top part of the oil for your prophets; or, if there are no prophets, for the poor. And look through your own clothes and other possessions, and pick out the best, and offer these to the prophets, or, if there are no prophets, to the poor.

DIDACHE: CHAPTER 13

VII   APPOINT for yourselves pastors and other leaders who are worthy of the Lord. They should be humble of heart; they should not love money; they should be honest, and their behavior blameless; and they should know firmly the truth revealed of God in Jesus Christ. Remember that their task is to supervise every spiritual ministry amongst you, so they must be able to distinguish true teaching from false teaching, true guidance from false. Never show contempt for those whom you have chosen as pastors, but treat them with honor. Yet do not rely on the pastors alone to reprove sin. Whenever anyone sees another sinning, he should have the courage to speak out, not in anger, but in peace. And when it is known that a person has done wrong to his neighbor, you should not speak to that sinner until he has repented.

DIDACHE: CHAPTER 15

VIII ON the Lord's Day, first confess your sins to one another. Let any of you that have quarreled talk to one another, and reconcile your difference. To worship God in a spirit of mutual enmity is to defile yourselves and to dishonor God. Then come together, break bread and hold the eucharist. Do not become lax, but ensure that the eucharist is celebrated every week. And gather frequently for prayer during the other days of the week. By gathering together for prayer, and also to hear teaching that is profitable for your soul, you will strengthen yourselves spiritually for the hour when the Lord comes to reign. As that hour approaches, many false prophets will appear; love between friends will turn to hate; sheep will become wolves. At that time you shall need every ounce of spiritual strength to withstand temptation and to hold fast to God.

DIDACHE: CHAPTERS 14 & 16

EPISTLE
to DIOGNETUS

THIS anonymous letter is the earliest surviving example of "apologetics," in which the writer attempts to justify the Christian faith before the pagan world. In its earliest days, the main concern of the Church was to win converts and establish some form of organization. But by the middle decades of the second century, Christianity had become a major religious element in many Roman cities, attracting wealthy and educated converts as well as the poor and dispossessed. Thus the authorities grew increasingly hostile, and local persecutions became more frequent and bloody. Scholarly Christians responded by trying to show that Christianity was rational and also constituted no threat to civil order; indeed, they argued that in practice the high moral standards of Christians would make the task of government easier.

Jesus being displayed to the hostile crowd
before his crucifixion in a painting by
Quentin Massys (c. 1466–1530).

I

SINCE I perceive, most excellent Diognetus, that you are exceedingly eager to learn the religion of the Christians, and are asking very clear and careful questions about them, I must respond. You have asked who is the God in whom they believe; how they worship him; why they show such disregard for the things of the world and are happy to die; why they reject as idols those who are considered gods by the Greeks, and also reject the superstitions of the Jews; what is the nature of the love that binds them together; and why this new religion has sprung up at this time, and not before. I welcome and admire this eagerness in you to learn about the Christian religion; and I ask God, who gives the power both of speaking and of hearing, that he may guide me to speak and you to hear in such a way that it will be of great benefit to you. And if what you hear in any way upsets or offends you, I ask your forgiveness.

EPISTLE TO DIOGNETUS: CHAPTER 1

11   PLEASE clear yourself of all prejudice that mists your mind, and throw aside the traditional attitudes that deceive you, and become like a child who is about to listen to a new story. Look, not only with your eyes, but also with your intelligence, at those entities that you call gods. What is their form; what is their substance? Is not one a stone, like the stones on that we walk; another a lump of bronze, no different from the vessels in that we carry water; another wood that is already rotting; another silver, requiring a man to guard it against theft; another iron, eaten by rust; another earthenware, no more beautiful than the plates on that we eat our meals? Are they not all made of perishable materials? Were they not forged by iron and fire? Did not the woodcarver make one, the brass-founder another, the silversmith another, the potter another? Before they were molded into their present shapes, was it not possible that they could have been given different shapes? Are they not all dumb, blind, without feelings, without souls, without movement? Do you call these things gods? Are these what you serve?

EPISTLE TO DIOGNETUS: CHAPTER 2

III

This is the reason why you hate Christians: that they do not treat as gods those pieces of wood and metal that you worship. While you are praising these lifeless objects, and vowing to serve them, the Christians despise them, and despise what you are doing. While you employ guards to prevent these objects from being stolen at night, the Christians mock your stupidity. And you hate their contempt and their mockery. Yet reflect on what you are doing. Imagine yourself in the position of one of your gods, being praised and worshipped and offered sacrifices of blood and burned fat. You would hate it and regard it as absurd. Yet you, surely, are worth much more than a lump of metal or wood. So why do you inflict this absurd behavior on these poor, lifeless objects? The metal, the wood, or the stone endures it because it can feel nothing. The victims are the worshippers, who make fools of themselves. Look at what you are doing, then you will understand why Christians refuse to serve such gods – which, in truth, are mere idols.

EPISTLE TO DIOGNETUS: CHAPTER 2

I V

THE distinction between Christians and other people lies not in country or language or customs. Christians do not dwell in special houses or districts of cities, nor do they use a peculiar dialect, nor do they have any extraordinary customs. Their teaching has not been discovered by the intellect or thought of clever men, nor do they advocate any human doctrine. Wherever they live they follow the local customs, eating the food that local people eat, living in ordinary houses, and wearing clothes indistinguishable from those of their neighbors. It is in their attitudes that they are distinctive. They live in the lands where they were born, but see themselves not as owners of that land, but as sojourners; they are strangers on this earth. To them, every foreign land is like their fatherland, and every fatherland like a foreign land. They behave as perfect and upright citizens, according to the laws of the state they inhabit; but they see themselves as citizens of another state, the kingdom of God.

EPISTLE TO DIOGNETUS: CHAPTER 5

V

To put it succinctly, what the soul is within the body, Christians are within the world. The soul is spread through all parts of the body, and Christians throughout all the cities of the world. The soul dwells in the body, but is not of the body; in the same way, Christians live in the world, but are not of the world. The soul is invisible, and is guarded by a visible body; the Christian religion is invisible, yet Christians are recognized in the world for what they are. The flesh tries to corrupt the soul by making the soul a slave to its desires; so the world tries to corrupt Christians by making them renounce their faith and adopt the world's values. The soul loves the flesh that hates it; Christians love the people who hate them. The soul is enclosed in the body and thence sustains it; Christians are confined within the world, and the world is sustained by their prayers. The soul when it withstands temptation becomes stronger; Christians by withstanding persecution become more numerous.

EPISTLE TO DIOGNETUS: CHAPTER 6

V I

CHRISTIAN doctrine is not based on some earthly discovery, nor is it based on a process of rational deduction. Equally the Christian doctrine is not a mystery that only people of great intellect can understand. It is given by the almighty and all-creating God, who has implanted his Word in their hearts. He did this by sending his own agent, who had been the instrument by which he created the heavens and the earth, into the world in human form. This agent had at the beginning of time set the sun and moon on their courses, enclosed the sea in its bounds, fashioned the mountains and the valleys, and brought every living creature into existence. You might imagine that when this agent took human form, he might strike terror into people's hearts. On the contrary, he was meek and gentle, a man among men, who won their hearts not by force, but by persuasion. He did not pursue people, but called them. He did not judge them, but loved them. He did not threaten them, but blessed them.

EPISTLE TO DIOGNETUS: CHAPTER 7

VII

WHAT else could cover our sins but the divine righteousness of God's Son? How else could our sins be wiped clean, except by God's Son taking upon himself our punishment? What a sweet exchange! What a wonderful event! What undeserved blessings! What a miracle that our wickedness should be absorbed by the One who is perfectly righteous, making us righteous! God allowed us to remain in the mire of our sin for so long to prove to us that in our own strength we could not lift ourselves. And when we were convinced that we needed help – when pride in our strength had been finally destroyed by our desperate plight – then he sent the greatest help that he could, in the form of his Son. Now a person only has to turn towards God's Son, and God's Son reaches down and lifts that person out of the mire of sin into the firm and solid ground of righteousness. And God's Son becomes to all those who turn to him their nurse, teacher, brother, counsellor, physician, and saviour, giving them strength, wisdom, love, comfort, power, and glory.

EPISTLE TO DIOGNETUS: CHAPTER 9

VIII   IF you also desire this faith, and so come to know God
as your Father, then you need only to turn towards his
Son. God created this world out of love for mankind,
putting all things under mankind's dominion; and he
gave us the faculty of reason, by which we can exercise
our dominion with justice and care. And in giving us
reason, he was fashioning us in his own image, for God
possesses supreme and perfect reason. Yet in our
sinfulness our image became distorted, and we failed to
use our reason justly and carefully. Then God sent his
Son to reveal himself, and thus show us the image of how
he created us and how he wishes to restore us. So when
you turn to God's Son you know who you truly are, and
how your true nature can be restored. And when you
come to know your true self through God's Son, you
shall be filled with joy beyond imagination, because you
shall know the completeness of God's love for you and
for all mankind.

EPISTLE TO DIOGNETUS: CHAPTER 10

JUSTIN

JUSTIN spent his early life studying philosophy under a variety of teachers, but found no satisfaction in their ideas. Then, in his middle years, he decided to study the new Christian religion, and quickly realized that it answered his deepest questions. Soon after his conversion he moved to Rome, where he set himself up as a Christian philosopher and invited pupils to study under him. His message was that Christianity did not refute the ancient wisdom of Plato and Aristotle, but was its fulfilment. His most famous work is his Apology, in which he seeks to show that Christianity is both rational in its thinking and noble in its morality. He also taught that God's Word is already present in every human soul; and those who live according to its truth, even if they are ignorant of the incarnation of the Word in Christ, will be saved. Justin was martyred for refusing to offer sacrifices to the pagan gods.

An altarpiece from the fifteenth century showing Christ crucified with the saints in attendance (Francesco di Stefano Pesellino, c. 1422–57).

I

To the Emperor and his son, to Lucius the philosopher, to the Senate and to all the Roman people. I write on behalf of a particular group, whose members are to be found in every part of the Empire. They are unjustly hated and reviled; and, as a member myself, I have drawn up this plea and petition. Philosophers, and all those who are pious and righteous, honor and cherish the truth; and they refuse to follow the ideas handed down to them from the past, merely because time has honored those ideas. Equally, such people neither behave unjustly, nor teach others to do so; those who love truth always speak and act justly, even at the risk of their own lives. So you, who are known for your piety and your devotion to the truth, will at least hear what we have to say. In these pages I will not use flattery, nor write things to win your favor. I ask you to judge my words according to the highest standards of reason and philosophy. We beg you to put aside all prejudice, and to forget all the rumors about us that you have heard; listen to us with an open mind.

JUSTIN'S APOLOGY: CHAPTERS 1 & 2

I I

W E know that many people regard us as criminals. We ask that any charges against us be thoroughly investigated. If they are found to be true, let us be punished accordingly. But if nothing can be found against us, then truth itself would not allow you to wrong us, simply on the basis of wicked rumors; or, if you were to pass sentence on us, it would be a judgment against yourselves. Every honorable man will recognize this as a fair challenge. Our way of life is open for all to see, and we are happy to give an honest account of ourselves to anyone who asks. Equally, we ask that your judgment about us be open, with an account of your reasons for approving or punishing us open for all to see. Indeed, when rulers make judgments in which the causes are public and open to scrutiny, both ruler and subjects gain. As one of the ancient philosophers said: "Unless both rulers and subjects become lovers of wisdom, cities cannot prosper." People blame us out of ignorance; we ask you to inspect us closely, and judge us justly.

JUSTIN'S APOLOGY: CHAPTER 3

III

GIVING a name to a group means nothing; what matters are the actions associated with that name. We are accused of being Christian. To us, that name is beautiful, implying grace and love; the true Christian is incapable of acting dishonestly or hatefully. To others, the name is evil; and if someone confesses to being a Christian, that itself is taken as grounds for punishment. But this puts us in an impossible position. If we deny being Christians, then we are denying the faith that fills us with divine grace; but if we confess to being Christians, we are punished for crimes that we could not possibly have committed. We ask you to ignore the name, and look instead at the lives of those to whom that name is ascribed. I have to acknowledge there are some describing themselves as Christian who believe in such a godless and criminal manner that they deserve to be punished. But do not judge us all by those traitors. Indeed, one can find people professing to be disciples of Zeus who are equally lawless. Judge us by those who sincerely seek to follow the teachings of Jesus Christ.

JUSTIN'S APOLOGY: CHAPTER 4

I V   WE regard the statues and other sacred objects that people put in temples as lifeless and dead; nor do they represent the true God. So we cannot honor these objects with sacrifices and garlands. You do not need us to tell you that these objects are fashioned by  craftsmen, who scrape, cut, mold, and beat their materials. And sometimes they take quite ordinary vessels and turn them into sacred objects. To treat things made by craftsmen as divine is an insult to God, whose glory and form cannot be captured by human imagination. The craftsmen who make these objects are themselves impure, so the things they produce cannot be pure and holy. Indeed, it is quite possible that a craftsman who corrupts the slave-girls who work with him produces objects to be put in temples and worshipped. How can any rational person treat a material object with reverence? And how can any rational person believe that God needs our sacrifices and garlands? God cannot be represented by any material object; and God is above all material needs, because he created the natural universe.

JUSTIN'S APOLOGY: CHAPTER 9

V

GOD only wants one thing from us: that we live according to his laws. And he has shown us how to do this by putting his Son on earth in human form. Thus by imitating the example of Christ we offer to God all the worship he requires. This means practicing all the virtues that the ancient philosophers have taught, and for our behavior to be inspired by love for all people. God created us and created the whole universe. Thus it is perfectly natural for us to practice virtue and to love one another; and to practice vice, and to be inwardly corrupt, is utterly unnatural. If we had brought ourselves into being, then it would be a matter of our own choice as to what is right and wrong. To have such an attitude is to be truly godless; and it is an attitude that the worship of material objects encourages. After all, to worship an object made by a craftsman is to worship man, not God. But we know that God has determined what is good and evil, right and wrong. And so by practicing the good and rejecting the evil, we are worshipping God.

JUSTIN'S APOLOGY: CHAPTER 10

V I

WHEN you hear that we look for a kingdom, you rashly imagine that we mean something merely human. But we mean a kingdom of which God is ruler. This surely becomes clear when we are put on trial and prove ourselves willing to die for the kingdom. If it were a human kingdom that we looked for, we would deny it in order to save our lives, and we would try to remain in hiding in order to obtain the things we looked for. But since we do not place our hopes in the present order, we are not troubled by being put to death. We are, in fact, of all men your best allies and helpers in securing peace and harmony on earth, since we believe that those who are wicked or malicious cannot hide themselves from God, and that God will punish people for their evil actions. If we were free to persuade everyone of this truth, then all crime and subversion would disappear. By putting their faith in God's kingdom, where people enjoy spiritual prosperity for all eternity, they would no longer want to cheat or steal to obtain greater material prosperity for themselves. They would restrain their evil desires and act only on good and holy impulses.

JUSTIN'S APOLOGY: CHAPTER 11

VII

CHRIST tells us not to quarrel with those who disagree with us. Ill-tempered argument can never win anyone's heart or mind, but only antagonize them. It is rather by our gentleness and generosity of spirit that we can put evil people to shame and win over those who are seeking the truth. There are many who were once violent and tyrannical, but are now models of patience and charity, because they were so impressed by the example of Christian neighbors. They observed how Christians refused to resist violence with violence, but instead showed love towards their enemies; and they saw how Christians were always honest and straight in their dealings with others. Moreover, they perceived the profound joy and serenity that such love and honesty bring to the soul, and they wanted to share that joy. In every nation there are such people, who were once on your side and are now on ours. We do not boast of any victory over you, but rather over the power of evil; and we ask you also to participate in that victory.

JUSTIN'S APOLOGY: CHAPTER 16

VIII THOSE of your subjects who cling to the old religion often try to escape paying the taxes that you decree. But the Christians are most assiduous in paying their taxes fully, because this is what Christ taught. This does not mean that we worship you as a deity, as many of your subjects do. On the contrary, we worship God alone. But in material matters we gladly serve you, recognizing you as rightful rulers appointed by God and subject to him; and we pray that you will come to acknowledge God as your ruler. If you dismiss our prayers as useless, and pay no attention to our frank statements about everything, it will not injure us, since we are convinced that you will ultimately be required to give an account of your actions to God. It is for your sake, not for our own, that we pray for you to recognize Christ as king of kings, and so participate in the salvation that he offers to all people. Death comes to all, even emperors; and thus we ask you, even now, to prepare for death by submitting your authority to that of Christ.

JUSTIN'S APOLOGY; CHAPTER 17

X

ATHENAGORAS

ATHENAGORAS was a man of wealth and position, who owned slaves and was loyal to the imperial order. But he was also rigorously honest, and after much reflection came to the conclusion that the teachings of Christ and his apostles were true. Like Justin, he saw no contradiction between Christianity and traditional philosophy, but believed that the new faith answered all the old philosophical questions. In his Apology, written to the emperor in about A.D. 180, he stressed his commitment to the empire and argued that the spread of Christianity was helping to promote peace and harmony in the cities. By this period, the main charges against Christians were incest, cannibalism, and atheism; Athenagoras demolished all three, showing that belief in God assures the good behavior of Christians.

Detail from a painting showing the poor man described in the Book of Ecclesiastes whose piety saved a city from destruction (Evelyn de Morgan, 1850–1919).

There was a little city and few men within it, and there came a great king against it, and besieged it, and built great bulwarks against it. Now there was found in it a poor wise man, and he by his wisdom delivered the city; yet no man remembered that same poor man. ...Wisdom is better than strength nevertheless the poor man's wisdom is despised, and his words are not heard.

I To Marcus Aurelius Anthoninus, emperor and – what is more important – philosopher. In your empire, different people observe different laws and customs; and no one is hindered by law or fear of punishment from devotion to his ancestral ways, even if they are ridiculous. A citizen of Troy calls Hector a god, and also worships Hales. Athenians perform religious rites and celebrate mysteries in honor of Pandora, who they imagine to be guilty of impiety for opening the box. The Egyptians count among their gods even cats, crocodiles, serpents, asps, and dogs. In brief, among every nation and people, men perform whatever sacrifices and mysteries they wish. And to all these cults you and the law grant toleration. You regard it as impious and wicked to believe in no god at all; you want everyone to worship the god he pleases, in order to be deterred from wrong-doing for fear of divine punishment. As a result, everyone admires your mildness, gentleness, and your peaceful and kindly attitude, and they rejoice that you give everyone equal rights under the law. Through your wisdom, the whole empire is at peace.

ATHENAGORAS' APOLOGY: CHAPTER 1

11 **B**UT the same toleration is not shown towards us who are called Christians. We do no wrong; and, as we shall show, we are of all men most law-abiding and loyal towards your empire. Yet you allow us to be harassed, plundered, and persecuted, and you let the mob make war on us because of our name. Thus we venture to state our case before you. From what we say, you will gather that we suffer unjustly, and that it is our persecutors, not we ourselves, who are breaking the law. Hence we ask you to devise measures to prevent our being victims of fake accusations. The injury we suffer from our persecution does not concern our property or our civil rights or any such matters. We hold these things in contempt, although they appear important to the crowd. We do not return blow for blow, nor do we sue those who rob and plunder us. But to those who hit us on one cheek, we offer the other cheek; and to those who steal our coats, we offer our shirts as well. Yet when we have given up our property, they plot against our souls and bodies, pouring upon us a multitude of accusations without the slightest foundation.

ATHENAGORAS' APOLOGY: CHAPTER 1

III   IF anyone can convict us of wrongdoing, be it trifling
         or more serious, we do not ask to escape punishment,
but we are prepared to pay the penalty, however cruel and
pitiless it may be. But if the accusation goes no further
than giving us the name "Christian" – and it is clear that
many ignorant people have been persuaded by false
rumors that all Christians are criminals – then it is your
duty, as a just and learned emperor, to protect us. Like so
many others in the cities and towns of the world, we
would then have good reason to be grateful to you. It is
an outrage, not only against us but against you, too, that
calling people by a particular name should brand them as
criminals. No name is of itself good or bad; it is the
actions associated with a name that matter. You know
that better than anyone, since you are such
a cultured man, well-versed in
philosophy. That is why innocent people
brought to trial before you, however
serious the charges, take courage; they know
that justice will prevail. We ask only the same
treatment as everyone else; to be judged by our
actions, not by our name.

ATHENAGORAS' APOLOGY: CHAPTER 2

I V

ET me state the charges that, as I understand it, are brought against us: atheism, holding cannibalistic feasts, and incest. If any of these are true, have no mercy on us; destroy us utterly, along with our wives and children, as unfit to inhabit the earth. To be guilty of those charges would be to have sunk lower than the lowest animal. Wild beasts do not attack and eat their own kind, nor do they have intercourse with members of their own family. They are also grateful to those who come to their aid; so if they had intelligence to know that God created and sustains them, they would believe and worship him. So there is no punishment severe enough to punish these crimes. But if these charges are inventions and unfounded slanders, they arise because it is natural for vice to oppose virtue, and it is according to God's law for evil and righteousness to battle against each other. We have no secrets; our lives are totally open to examination; we wish to hide nothing from your scrutiny, or from the scrutiny of our neighbors. Indeed, we are confident that the more people see the divine grace at work within us, the more they will be inclined to adopt our faith.

ATHENAGORAS' APOLOGY: CHAPTER 3

V

I WILL reply to the charges one by one. We are not, of course, atheists; indeed, it seems silly to have to answer such an allegation. There are people who are genuinely atheistic, such as Diagoras, who chopped up a statue of Hercules for firewood to boil his turnips; he proclaims publicly that God does not exist. To be an atheist is to make no distinction between the material and the spiritual realms, the temporal and eternal. But we clearly distinguish God from matter. God is uncreated, infinite, and eternal, to be grasped only by pure mind and intelligence; while all material things were created by God, and are infinite and perishable. If we shared the views of Diagoras when we have so many reasons to praise God – for the order, harmony, greatness, color, form, and organization of the world – then we would rightly be regarded as mad, as well as criminal. But our teaching affirms one God, who existed from before time began, and who will exist beyond the end of time. He made all things through his Word, the son, who is the agent of all creation. Thus it is not we, but our accusors, who should be treated as mad.

ATHENAGORAS' APOLOGY: CHAPTER 4

V I

To grasp the rational basis of our faith, that from the beginning there was one God who created the universe, consider the position if this were not so. Imagine that originally there were two or more gods. Either they would have to share in one and the same being, or else they would be independent from each other. If they shared in one and the same being, they would, in fact, be a single God. It may be argued that these gods were like different parts of a single entity, as the hands, eyes, and feet are different parts of the body. But this is impossible, because God is infinite and eternal, and thus cannot be divided up into parts. If, on the other hand, the gods are independent, there would inevitably be a hierarchy of gods, since the one who created the universe would be above all the others. In this case, the second and third gods must exist outside the universe, and are thus no concern of ours; or inside the universe, so that they are themselves creatures of the supreme God.

ATHENAGORAS' APOLOGY: CHAPTER 8

VII   THERE are all sorts of wicked and unfounded rumors of immorality amongst us. The moral teaching that we espouse is not our own invention, but comes from God. And it can be summarized very simply: "Love your enemies, bless those who curse you, and pray for those who curse you, that you may be sons of your Father in heaven." These precepts are often ridiculed as absurd nonsense by those who despise us. Yet I can show you simple, uneducated people – laborers, tradesmen, old women – who put these principles into practice, and as a consequence are radiant with joy. These people cannot make great speeches to explain their faith, but their good deeds speak louder than any speech. When struck, they do not strike back; when robbed, they do not sue; to those who ask, they give; and they love their neighbors as themselves. Such morality cannot be practiced by human power alone; it requires the heart to be purified by God. Thus day by day those who follow the Christian way must pray to God to be made pure and holy.

ANTHENAGORAS' APOLOGY: CHAPTER 11

VIII W E speak of God in three ways: as the Father; as his Word, the Son; and as the Holy Spirit. They are united in power. The Son is the intelligence, reason, and wisdom of the Father; the Spirit is an effluence, like light from fire. In the same way, we recognize that there are other powers that surround matter and pervade it. Of these, there is one in particular that is hostile to God. By this we do not mean that there is anything fundamentally opposed to God, as some other religions teach, because if anything did manage to set itself up against God, it would cease to exist: it would be crushed into pieces by the power and might of God. Rather, we mean that the spirit that inhabits matter is hostile to God's goodness. This goodness is an essential quality of God, as inseparable from him as color is inseparable from an object and cannot exist without it. As red is fused with fire, and blue with sky, so goodness is fused with God. Yet God created a hostile spirit in matter, in order to challenge us with the choice between good and evil.

ATHENAGORAS' APOLOGY: CHAPTER 12

XI

IRENAEUS

IRENAEUS was born in Asia Minor in about A.D. 130, and as a young man saw and heard Polycarp of Smyrna. He traveled to Gaul, where he became bishop of the church in Lyons. He is often described as the first biblical theologian. Whereas the apologists saw the Bible as the source from which a rational philosophy could be derived, Irenaeus took the Old Testament and the gospels as the record of God's action in history in which, God revealed his nature and will. Thus the task of the Christian writer is not to invent theological doctrines, but to expound the Bible. To Irenaeus, the great enemies of the faith were the Gnostics, both because they loved theological speculation, and, more fundamentally, because they denied the presence of God in external events and objects. More vigorously than any of the other Early Fathers, he asserted the goodness of all creation, seeing in every living creature the reflection of God's love.

A sixteenth-century Russian icon depicting Elijah being taken up to heaven in a fiery chariot.

I   CERTAIN men who have rejected the truth are
spreading amongst us false stories and doctrines,
which are causing division rather than building up our
faith in God. With their crafty rhetoric they lead astray
those who are new to the faith, and then capture their
minds with distorted versions of our Lord's teaching,
corrupting his beautiful words. These evil people pretend
they have a direct knowledge of the One who created and
ordered the universe, claiming that God has revealed
secret truths about himself and his heavenly kingdom.
With their smooth tongues they convince simple-minded
people of their spiritual authority, and they persuade
them that they, too, can gain this secret knowledge if
they obey their commands. Thus these haters of truth
turn good, honest Christians into their slaves, who will
believe whatever they say and do whatever they order.
Their poor followers, who sincerely wish to know the
truth, do not realize that their minds and hearts are being
stuffed with lies.

IRANAEUS AGAINST HERESIES: PART 1, CHAPTER 1

11   THE Church is now scattered over the whole
civilized world to the ends of the earth. But it was
founded in a particular place at a particular time by a
particular person, Jesus Christ. And he appointed apostles
to teach the world that there is one God, the Father
almighty, who made heaven and earth and sea and all
that lives in them; that he, Jesus Christ, is the Son of
God, made flesh for our salvation; and that through the
Holy Spirit all people may be led to know him as their
Lord. The apostles also related the full story of Jesus
Christ: his birth by a virgin; his suffering and
resurrection from the dead; and his ascension into
heaven. And they taught that he will return from heaven
to restore all things to perfection, and to raise up the
whole human race, so that all may bend their knee to
him in adoration, and acknowledge him as King of the
universe. At that time, all those who have
rejected him, or who first accepted him
and then under pressure turned
away from him, will be banished
and sent into the eternal fire of
hell. But the righteous and holy,
who have kept his commandments
and remained in his love, will be
clothed in eternal glory.

IRENAEUS AGAINST HERESIES: PART 1, CHAPTER 10

III HAVING received its faith from the apostles, the Church carefully preserves it. Although it is scattered across the world, the Church spiritually lives in one house. So she believes the truth with one heart and one soul, and preaches and teaches the truth as if she had one mouth. And although the languages of the world are many and various, the meaning of the Church's tradition is one and the same. The churches that have been established in Germany share the faith of the churches in Iberia; Christians in Egypt and Libya are spiritual brothers of Christians in the Celtic lands. As the same sun shines in every part of the world, so the same truth, handed down by the apostles, illuminates the minds and hearts of people everywhere. Anyone who wishes to know the truth can receive the same light. The test of a true Christian teacher is that he wishes only to pass on to others what he himself heard, without addition, subtraction, or amendment. He may possess great powers of oratory, which make people more eager to listen to him; but these powers are put at the service of truth.

IRANAEUS AGAINST HERESIES: PART 1, CHAPTER 10

IV C HRISTIANS vary greatly in their understanding of the truth. Some have a deep appreciation of our faith, while others still are quite shallow in their faith. But it is the same ocean in which they are peering, the same truth that they are seeking to comprehend. It was in order to reach people at every level that our Lord spoke in parables. Those with shallow understanding could enjoy the parables as simple stories with moral lessons that they could learn; while those with deeper faith could penetrate the divine mysteries with these tales and images. By the parables and other teaching, our Lord invited people into a new covenant with God. Our side of the covenant is to obey God's commandments and love God's creatures as fully as our understanding allows. God's side of the covenant is to pour out his blessing both on earth and in heaven, so that we can share in his glory. This covenant was sealed with the blood of our Lord, who suffered and died on the cross for our sake. His suffering, his death, and then his resurrection together form the supreme parable, which, if understood fully, reveals the fullness of God.

IRENAEUS AGAINST HERESIES: PART 1, CHAPTER 10

V

LET us now look clearly at the leader of these men
who distort the truth, and lay bare the
inconsistencies of his teaching. His name is Valentinus,
and he has adopted the teachings of the Gnostics of
Christianity. He claims that there is a complex hierarchy
of spiritual beings, at the top of which are two beings,
one called the Father and the other called Truth. He also
says that there is a spiritual Mother, who conceived a
Son; and the Son has been appointed to rule the world.
Thus the Son is not made of flesh, but is purely spiritual;
the appearance of flesh is purely an illusion. It follows
from this that the Son did not – and does not – share our
temptations, and cannot suffer; and this means that the
crucifixion was a fraud, in which the spiritual Son simply
appeared to suffer, but in fact felt nothing. If this were
the case, he did not take upon himself the punishment
for sin that we deserved; and so we have not been
redeemed from sin. Valentinus claims that by claiming
Jesus is purely spiritual, he is asserting his true divinity,
since God could not be made flesh. But in fact he is
turning God's plan for the salvation of mankind into an
evil joke.

IRENAEUS AGAINST HERESIES: PART 1, CHAPTER 11

V I

WHEN it comes to the resurrection, the teaching of Valentinus becomes both most attractive and most evil. Many find it difficult to believe that God could take upon himself human form, and yet when they hear about the works and the teachings of Jesus, they are convinced he is divine. But it is even more difficult to accept that when his human flesh was killed on the cross, that same flesh could rise to life. Valentinus, of course, claims that the resurrection is purely spiritual; that when the disciples saw the risen Christ, his human form had no substance, but was merely the way in which his spirit was made manifest to them. Indeed, since Christ never had human form, he never died; and the resurrection is the proof of this. How tempting it is to believe such a doctrine. We do not have to accept the scandal of God being murdered as a criminal, nor do we have to accept the miracle of dead flesh being brought back to life. Yet if that were true, why should we be disciples? If God never became flesh, like us, he could neither redeem us nor reveal to us his promise of eternal life. It is only by becoming like us that God can make us like him, restoring us in his image.

IRENAEUS AGAINST HERESIES: PART 1, CHAPTER 12

VII   ALL of us have at times been tempted to mutilate the gospel, picking out the parts that suit us and cutting out the rest. But it is not for us to create the religion that pleases us; rather, we must accept the faith that God gives us in its entirety. The haters of the truth, by contrast, are happy to pick and choose their beliefs. One of them, Marcion, utterly mutilates Luke's gospel, removing everything about the birth of our Lord as well as all the words of our Lord that, either directly or by implication, affirm his Father as the creator of the universe. His reason for doing this is that he teaches the existence of two Gods: an evil God who created the material world, which brings suffering and misery, and a good God who creates the spiritual world, including human souls. He says that Christ is the Son of the good God, who is at war with the evil God. Such a view has many attractions, the greatest of which is that it suggests that we can escape all suffering and misery by making our souls utterly indifferent to our bodily state. Indeed, it is this notion that lies at the root of this teaching; and thus I shall seek to refute it in depth, by describing in detail our true faith.

IRENAEUS AGAINST HERESIES: PART 1, CHAPTER 27

VIII THE gospels contain the true plan of our salvation. Those who wrote the gospels were either witnesses themselves to what they describe, or received their information from witnesses. After our Lord left the earth and sent down his Holy Spirit, they traveled across the world, preaching the good news; and later they wrote down a full account for future generations. These accounts are thus the foundation and pillar of our faith, on which we can depend completely. Some have said that these men were imperfect when they preached and wrote, so we cannot rely on the gospels; indeed, it is even suggested that we should ask people today who are spiritually perfect to correct the gospels. This is not only arrogant, but also profoundly mistaken. The perfection of the gospels does not rest on the perfection of those who wrote them; no one in this world can claim perfection. We can rely on the gospels because the Holy Spirit, sent by Christ himself, guided the hands of the writers. Thus even the apparent inconsistencies and factual contradictions are put there by the Holy Spirit; it is not for us to argue with what we read, but to try to understand what it means and why it was written.

IRENAEUS AGAINST HERESIES: PART 3, CHAPTER 2

TERTULLIAN

THE apologists and even Irenaeus wanted to proclaim Christianity in ways that were acceptable to Greek thought. Tertullian, by contrast, rejected all philosophy as false, believing that God's revelation in Christ overturned all previous ideas, and, far from indulging in rational speculation, Christians should rely for guidance directly on the Holy Spirit. Paradoxically, Tertullian argued his case with the elegance and logic of the finest philosopher. He was born in Carthage in North Africa in the middle of the second century and became a successful lawyer. He converted to Christianity in the year 193 after witnessing the courage of Christians facing torture and death for their faith. Thereafter, books and tracts on every aspect of Christianity poured from his pen. And although his prose is at times convoluted, and his arguments obscure, it is uplifted by his fiery passion for Christ.

A Young Man at Prayer
by Hans Memling (1425-1494).

I   L ET us consider Christ's precept that we should pray in secret. Of course, God has eyes and ears everywhere, so whenever a man prays, God can see and hear him. When we pray in secret we gain no worldly respect for our devotion, so the only motive for praying secretly is the love of God himself. Equally, we do not have the pleasure of the company of other people, so the only pleasure is the company of God himself. Thus when we pray in secret, our motive and our desire is pure. Let us also consider Christ's precept that we should pray simply, with few words. We should never imagine that when we speak to God, we are telling him anything he does not know already. The benefit from expressing ourselves in prayer is for ourselves, not for God. Through prayer we come to trust in God for all things, and we align our own will with his. Thus before we pray, we should consider carefully our true needs, and reflect deeply on his will. We shall realize that our needs are few, and his commands are simple. When we come to pray, therefore, we shall find that only a few words are necessary.

TERTULLIAN ON PRAYER: CHAPTER 1

I I LET us now consider the model of prayer the Lord gave us, which contains almost the whole of his teaching. It begins with a proclamation of faith: "Our Father in heaven." The Lord frequently declared God to be our Father, and he even said that we should call no one on earth "father," saving the title for God alone. The name indicates both his love for us and his power. He treats us with the love that a human father treats his children. But unlike a human father whose power to protect and care for his son is limited, God's power is infinite; so we as his children can depend on him totally. We remember the extraordinary privilege we enjoy in being able to speak to God as Father. Others, such as Moses, have yearned to know his name. But only in Christ do we come to know him as our loving parent, and can enjoy speaking to him in prayer with the same intimacy that a child speaks to his father and mother. And when we add "Hallowed be your name," we are asking that we who use the name "Father" may be made holy. Christ commands us to be holy as our Father in heaven is holy; and we repeat that command in this simple phrase.

TERTULLIAN ON PRAYER: CHAPTER 2

III   THE next phrase, "Your will be done in heaven and on earth" does not imply that God's will could be thwarted by human opposition. On the contrary, if God chose to impose his will, then even the most powerful emperor in the world could not stand against it. Yet God gives us the freedom to choose, and so he restrains his power. Thus in using this phrase, we are asking God to guide our wills, so that our desires and actions are in accordance with his will. The word "earth" in this phrase does not just refer to the world, but refers also to our bodies; and the word "heaven" does not denote only God's heavenly home, but also our souls, because our souls belong in heaven. Thus we are asking God that our bodily desires should not choke the soul, as weeds can choke a plant. Rather, we ask that the body should desire only those deep things that sustain its health and strength, and so be a beautiful and pure temple for the soul. In this way, our every word and action will reflect the glory of God himself.

TERTULLIAN ON PRAYER: CHAPTER 3

I V   How finely is God's wisdom shown in the arrangement of the Lord's prayer. After petitions for heavenly things, a petition for earthly needs is added: "Give us this day our daily bread." Yet even this petition must be understood in heavenly terms. Christ tells us to seek first his kingdom, and that is why petitions for the kingdom come first; and he assures us that if we let God reign in our hearts, all our earthly needs will be met. Thus we do not even need to ask for literal bread; God will provide it. "Our bread" in this petition refers to Christ, because he is the bread of life. In asking for daily bread, we are pleading that Christ may perpetually live in us. This petition is truly that of children speaking to their father. A child is too simple to ask his father for spiritual things, but asks his father for his bodily needs; and his father provides for those needs. Likewise, we are too simple and stupid to know our spiritual needs; so we ask our heavenly Father for our bodily needs. But in this case the Father provides for our spiritual as well as our bodily needs.

TERTULLIAN ON PRAYER: CHAPTER 5

V   Having recognized the abundant generosity of God, it is fitting that we now recognize his abundant mercy, by asking him to "forgive our debts, as we forgive the debts of others." In order to offer this petition sincerely, we must first reflect on the full extent of our debts. These, of course, are not material, but spiritual and moral debts. Debt is a metaphor for sin, because when we do wrong, we are in debt to our victim to the value of the wrong we have done; and this debt is also owed to God as a fine, because he is the final judge. In our own power we can never repay our debts to God, so we plead with him to forgive the debts. Equally, we can never fully put right the wrong we have done to others, so we depend on their forgiveness also. For this reason we commit ourselves in this petition to mutual forgiveness; as God forgives us, so we forgive others and ask them to forgive others. Without forgiveness we are caught in a cycle of hatred and revenge, which can only end in mutual destruction. Forgiveness is the only gateway through which sinners can find peace and safety.

TERTULLIAN ON PRAYER: CHAPTER 6

V I   HAVING asked to be forgiven our sins, it is natural that we should want never to be tempted into sin in the future. So we ask God to "lead us not into temptation." These words seem to suggest that God might lead us into temptation, as if he actually wanted to corrupt us. That, of course, is unthinkable, because temptation and sin belong to the devil. Yet it is God who allows the devil to operate in the world. God has the power to destroy evil at a single stroke. He chooses not to do so, because he has given us freedom to choose; and this freedom implies that there is a possibility of evil, as well as of good, in the world. Thus we shall face temptation throughout our lives, until the end of time. But since the devil is ultimately under God's power, we can ask God that the temptations that we face should not be beyond our power of endurance. And God knows that by allowing the devil to tempt us in ways that, through prayer, we can endure, our faith will be strengthened. So this petition can be more fully expressed as: "Lead us not into temptation beyond our power of endurance." And in answering this prayer, God thus fulfils the final petition, to "deliver us from the devil."

TERTULLIAN ON PRAYER: CHAPTER 7

VII   OW should we prepare ourselves for prayer? The first and most important preparation is to make peace with our brothers. If there is any disagreement that has not been resolved, or misdemeanor that has not been confessed and forgiven, then we must seek to put such matters right as a matter of the utmost urgency. How can we dare to approach God if our consciences are uneasy and our hearts are restless? If we seek his mercy, when we have not sought to put right things that are wrong, then we must expect his anger. It is as if we were eating a meal with our hands still covered in dirt from the farmyard; far from nourishing our bodies, we would poison them. For that reason, we wash our hands before eating. Similarly, if our souls are encrusted with the dirt of sin and we have made no effort to wash ourselves clean of sin, prayer shall be a spiritual poison to us. Of course, even when we have washed ourselves spiritually, we remain capable of sin; so we approach God not as holy saints, but as humble, penitent sinners. And in prayer we plead with God to save us from further sin.

TERTULLIAN ON PRAYER: CHAPTERS 11 & 12

V I I I   It is good to pray in an orderly and humble fashion. This does not necessitate raising the hands high in the air, nor looking upwards to heaven. The hands may be raised slightly. The tone of the voice should be subdued. Since God loves the mind, not the sound that the mouth emits, there is no need to shout. Those who pray loudly disturb their neighbor and draw attention to themselves. Moreover, it is important to decide whether to reveal to others our petitions. In some cases, I may wish to tell others of my petitions, and ask them to pray with me. In other cases, my petitions may be private and personal, so it is appropriate for me to pray in silence.

TERTULLIAN ON PRAYER: CHAPTER 17

INDEX